EDUCATING GLOBALLY

GLOBALLY

CASE STUDY OF A GÜLEN-INSPIRED SCHOOL
IN THE UNITED STATES

EDUCATING GLOBALLY

CASE STUDY OF A GÜLEN-INSPIRED SCHOOL IN THE UNITED STATES

Erkan Acar

TUGHRA
BOOKS

New Jersey

Published by Tughra Books
345 Clifton Ave., Clifton,
NJ, 07011, USA

www.tughrabooks.com

Library of Congress Cataloging-in-Publication Data Available

ISBN: 978-1-59784-326-3

Printed by
İmak Ofset, İstanbul - Turkey

Contents

APPENDICES

Acknowledgements

I would like to express my deepest gratitude to my chair and advisor, Dr. Mary Salvaterra, from the College of Education and Human Development at Marywood University, for her guidance and patience. I would like to thank the committee members, Dr. Lois Draina, and Dr. Shamshad Ahmed especially for helping me to identify my research focus for my dissertation, which is published by Tughra Books. I would also like to thank them for the motivation, guidance and their timely feedback. My sincerest appreciation to my parents Adil and Emine Acar, for their unending patience, understanding, and support during my doctoral study. Finally, I am grateful that this research was supported in part by a Marywood University Graduate Student Research Award.

CHAPTER 1

Introduction

M any different educational ideas and practices have been implemented in schools throughout the world. Starting with Confucius whose ethical principles informed education in ancient China to Howard Gardner's "multiple intelligences" that resonate with educators today in the United States, each era has contributed to the philosophical foundation of educational philosophy worldwide. Educators continue to explore how these philosophies affect cognitive development (Nodding, 2007). There is no consensus on one single philosophy that is most effective in terms of developing overall intellectual maturity.

Furthermore, different philosophies form the foundation not only of general education, but also contribute pedagogical strategies in disciplines such as in teaching mathematics (Marlow, 1996), or in effective English instruction (Marlow, 1992).

The prevalence of historically divergent educational philosophies and beliefs is due to a system that constantly aims to improve the moral, cultural, political, and economic values of the times, as well as the differing opinions about what educational techniques are most effective in advancing the skills necessary for the betterment of the community.

The education system in the United States has been influenced by many philosophies since its inception during colonial days. At that time the idealism of Plato and the realism of Aristotle formed the basis of the educational system. With the spread of democracy and the explosion of scientific theories, the educational system within the

United States became as diverse as its people (Cohen, 1999). The history of American education is replete with examples of theorists who have had an influence on the growth of education. The importation of theories from Western nations include those of Rousseau and his concept of naturalism, Pestalozzi and Maria Montessori's ideas of early childhood education, and Froebel's formation of the kindergarten (Gutek, 2011). Statesmen such as Horace Mann, Thomas Jefferson, and Benjamin Franklin contributed to the advancement of education on American soil along with modern experimentalists John Dewey, Howard Gardner, and countless others who continue to find ways (critical thinking, differentiated instruction, constructivism) to educate children, women, blacks, immigrants, and other special needs students (Gutek, 2011).

In addition to theories driving the growth of public schools in America, private schools developed to preserve religious and cultural beliefs. The immigrant population from predominantly Catholic countries in the late 1800s and 1900s spurred the growth of Catholic schools especially in the anti-Catholic climate of those times. A philosophy based on Catholic beliefs did not, however, exclude curricular and pedagogical advancements. Catholic schools in the U.S. share a Judeo-Christian vision as an educational philosophy. Such schools have a commitment to the developing faith of students with Catholic/Christian perspectives. Accordingly their curriculum, school activities and policies are designed around a Catholic perspective with respect to the general obligations required by the state, such as equality in education and respect for diversity (McDermott, 1997).

Lutheran schools in the Unites States a similar commitment to the developing faith of their students. According to Lutheran Schools of America (n.d.) the mission of the Lutheran Schools are "to establish Christian, confessionally Lutheran, community based schools which are characterized by academic excellence, high student achievement, and community service". Whether Catholic or protestant, denominational private schools are Bible-centered and Gospel-oriented schools that also follow the standard rules and regulations of every school in the United States.

Both Hasidic schools and Islamic schools also have their foundation in their cultural values and commitment to the principles of their beliefs. Jewish and Muslim parents, like Catholic parents in the early 1900s, sought religious freedom and safety in their own schools. After the tragedy of September 11, 2001, Muslim parents wanted a safe educational haven for their children to overcome the resultant backlash of hatred and bigotry (Cainkar, 2009).

Gülen-inspired schools are a recent example of private schools in the United States that follow a unique educational philosophy. The educational philosophy of Gülen-inspired schools is based on four elements: altruism, accepting and appreciating the teaching as a noble action/vocation, synthesis between science and religious values, and the cooperation among the stakeholders (Aslandogan & Cetin, 2007). Although not classified as Islamic schools, Islam may be the driving influence behind Gülen-inspired schools' approach to education and to life.

Purpose of the Study

The purpose of this case study is to describe the characteristics of a Gülen-inspired School (GIS) in the United States. The study identifies the characteristics of a U.S. based GIS in terms of the school's curriculum, history, success, hiring practices, admissions process, and networking. In order to understand its unique meaning and significance, interviews and observations were conducted in one GIS located in the northeast region of the United States. For the purpose of anonymity this study refers to the school as GIS.

Research Question

How is the philosophy of a "Gülen-inspired school" reflected in a U.S. based GIS, as it relates to curriculum, history, success, hiring process, admission process, and networking?

Historical Background and Overview of GIS

The Gülen-inspired school described in this study is a private school founded in 1997 with 25 students and four teachers in the northeast region of the United States. Since that time, the number of students and teachers has increased every year. In its first year, GIS offered third, fourth and fifth grade education to its students. In the following years, the size of the student body and the number of grade levels increased. For instance, in the 2000-2001 academic year, the school had 55 students and started offering second, sixth, seventh and eigth grade instruction for its students. The student population of GIS increased to 160 in 2005. The school started offering all K-12 grades in the 2007-2008 academic years. In the 2010-2011 academic year, GIS had 257 students, 24 teachers and two administrators, and offers K-12 education in two separate buildings. The original GIS building was still in use, and offered pre-k to third grade education. A second building, first rented in 2003, housed middle school and high school classes.

On its web page, the GIS describes its mission as follows:

"The mission of [GIS] is to provide a well-rounded educational experience that will prepare students to confidently pursue the journey of their lives. In fulfilling its mission, [GIS] seeks to inspire a love of learning and to instill a strong sense of moral behavior. We strive to nurture the students' natural abilities while maintaining the belief that children need direction, discipline and standards of excellence to thrive.

[GIS] seeks an active partnership between school and family based on a shared commitment to the students' goals, values and the special joys of childhood. All members of the [GIS] community are asked to hold each other to high expectations of behavior and achievement so that our children will aspire to make a better world. Join us and be a part of a dynamic learning environment. We strive for excellence!"

GIS's current student body is 85% white, 10% black, and 5% other Academic achievement in the school was easily measurable. The graduation rate was 100% since 2008 when the first high school students of GIS graduated. Furthermore, all of the GIS's graduates are enrolled in four years colleges. In the 2010-2011 academic year, the average SAT score of GIS students was 1812 out of 2400. The state's average where the school is located was 1500. In addition, in the 2010-2011 academic year 75% of GIS's graduating seniors were accepted into the nation's top 50 colleges and universities, including Lehigh University, Duke University, University of California Los Angeles, University of Chicago, University of California Berkley, Georgetown University, New York University, Brandies University, Cornell University, and Penn State University. GIS's webpage indicates that GIS's students received substantial financial assistance. The total scholarship award average for the 2010-2011 academic years was $228,750.

GIS students have also received medals from various competitions (e.g., science Olympiads, art contests). Recent scholastic achievements by GIS students include: 2007 American Legion Art Contest, first place; 2007 Discovery Channel Contest, north division, five first places; 2007 Intel Engineering Contest, third place; 2008 New Jersey Science Olympiad, first place; and 2009 New Jersey Science Olympiad, fourth place.

GIS's buildings have modern equipment, such as projectors, classroom internet access, and fully-equipped laboratories in which courses in physics, chemistry, and biology are taught. GIS also has a multi-purpose area in the school that is used for sports activities, lectures, plays, and meetings. In addition, the classes were small in size with an average class size of 12 students.

Theoretical Framework

The theory of social capital may explain the apparent academic success of the GIS. Independent schools such as the GIS are privately funded. Studies about social capital and particularly its connection to education reveal that social capital increasingly has been recognized as a solution to current educational and social problems (Dika & Singh, 2002). Yet there seems to be no unanimous definition of social capital. Social capital is typically defined by its functions. These functions vary from definition to definition, but there are two elements that most definitions have in common: (a) some aspects of social structures, and (b) actors whose actions are facilitated within those social structures (Coleman, 1988).

Assumptions

For the purpose of this case study, it is assumed that the respondents answered the interview questions in an honest and unbiased way and their answers accurately represented their experiences at GIS. It is also assumed that the interview questions exposed meaningful information that is a reflection of people's experience with the school and reveal the philosophical foundation of Gülen-inspired school.

Significance of the Study

An in-depth qualitative study of a Gülen-inspired school contributes to the literature in the following way. Several scholars studied Gülen-inspired schools in different countries (Agai, 2005; Michel, 2005; Ozdalga, 2005; Akyol, 2008; Irvine, 2007; Kalyoncu, 2008). Most of these studies emphasized the schools' ability to adapt to new cultures and the educational systems of diverse countries. To the researcher's best knowledge, there is no similar case study of a Gülen-inspired school located in the United States published yet. This study will be the first case study for a U.S. based Gülen-inspired school. Analyzing a noticeably successful Gülen-inspired school in the U.S. may be beneficial not only for scholars but for politicians and educators who are seeking new strategies and applicable policies for the young generations. In other words, this specific Gülen-inspired school's education practices can benefit not only the public school system but also other private schools, including Gülen-inspired schools, around the world.

Definitions

Gülen-Inspired Schools

Gülen-inspired schools are those founded around the world by the volunteers of the Gülen Movement. Gülen-inspired schools provide all levels of education (K-12 and college levels) in different educational systems. Such schools follow Fethullah Gülen's educational philosophy.

Success

For this case study, success refers to (a) significant graduation rates, (b) significant college enrollment, and (c) significant test scores (e.g. SAT scores) of students in K-12 institutions.

School's Networks

The study will define school's networks with three dimensions: networks among parents, faculty and community members. Such networks can be sustained through activities such as conferences, meetings, workshops, mutual visits, and trips.

Limitations

An obvious limitation of this case study was the limited number of interviewees because of the few teachers and administrators currently employed at the school. A second limitation was the lack of reflection on the historical development of the school since some of the employees and students have left or graduated since its founding. Furthermore, due to the specific characteristics of the sample group and the region, this study and its conclusion cannot be generalized for other Gülen-inspired schools in the United States.

Interdisciplinary Nature of the Study

This qualitative case study, by its very nature, requires a holistic description of the Gülen-inspired school as an alternative school with an unconventional educational philosophy in the United States. Therefore, this study will use an interdisciplinary approach by focusing on the connections between parts of a whole – its educational practices, the implementation of its philosophy and its sociological concerns. Further, social capital that is used as the theoretical framework for this case study naturally brings an interdisciplinary perspective since the concept of social capital specifically focuses on the network among the individuals that promotes benefits for the societies in diverse disciplines (i.e., economy, education, and politics).

CHAPTER 2

Literature Review

In order to provide a comprehensive background for the case study, three specific aspects have been explained: (a) Fethullah Gülen as an educator, (b) Gülen Movement, (c) Gülen's educational philosophy and Gülen-inspired schools. Furthermore, under the title of Gülen Movement, two specific subtitles, Islam as a driving force and interparty dialogue, have been discussed.

Fethullah Gülen as an Educator

Fethullah Gülen was born in 1941 in a village in Erzurum, eastern Turkey. Gülen received his early education from his parents. This education mostly centered around religious education. At that time, general secular education for ordinary Turkish people was very limited. However, Gülen attended the nearest state primary school for three years. Gülen was unable to continue his secondary education since his father was assigned by the state as preacher and imam to another town where there was no secondary school. During Gülen's adolescent years, mosques and congregational prayers were allowed by the state. On the other hand, the state prohibited all other forms of religious practices. However, many Turkish people, like Gülen's parents, continued teaching the Turkish Islamic tradition including the Qur'an, basic religious practices, and prayer to their children. Like most people, Gülen's parents avoided conflicts with the new regime and its authorities. Instead, they concealed the fact that they were providing basic Islamic instruction to their own and their neighbors' children (Erdogan, 1996).

Gülen's primary education until 1950 was simply about Islam and primarily given by his parents. After 1950 when he was ten years old his educational life became more traditional since he did not continue formal education. During the 1950s, Gülen was instructed by various prominent religious scholars and completed his religious education. He received his traditional Islamic *ijaza* (license to teach) from those Sufi masters. Although many people were receiving their *ijaza* throughout this informal religious education, the state ignored and did not support this educational model (Erdogan, 1996). One of the most important teachers of Gülen was Muhammed Lütfi Efendi who was a Sufi master in the city of Erzurum. Gülen continued his education, especially spiritual and religious training, with him. Gülen also met with Bediüzzaman Said Nursi's students, and was introduced to the *Risale-i Nur*. This collection of books that are in one respect a complete and contemporary Islamic school of thought, contributed a great deal to Gülen's intellectual and spiritual development (Unal & Williams, 2000). Throughout external exams, Gülen completed his secondary level secular education. After receiving his secondary school diploma, Gülen passed special exams to become an imam and preacher. After passing the exams, he was assigned by the state to Edirne located in western Turkey (Erdogan, 1996).

Gülen's formal education was complete after he received his secondary level education diploma. Meanwhile, Gülen continued his modern education in science and philosophy. Further, he enhanced his intellect in other disciplines including literature and history. He also became interested in the modern sciences (e.g., physics, chemistry, biology, and astronomy). At the same time he read western philosophers that include Camus, Sartre, and Marcus. Gülen emphasizes that he also had the chance to read western classics during his military service in the city of Iskenderun. Since he was assigned to give lectures on faith and morality he had plenty of time to read western classics given by his commanding officer (Erdogan, 1996).

Gülen's service in the field of education started in the Kestane Pazari Qur'anic School in Izmir. His managerial responsibility included the mosque, the student study and boarding hall, and preaching in the regional mosques (Erdogan, 1996). According to Cetin (2010) during his Kestane Pazari years, Gülen's perspective on education and service to the community solidified. Coffee houses became one of the important meeting places where Gülen shared his ideas and thoughts in early 1970s. Gülen also lectured at villages and provinces in the region, and led one of the most important activities that he would organize, a summer camps for students.

With Gülen's encouragement, ordinary people started to mobilize collective efforts, especially in the field of education. In 1978, the first university preparation center in Manisa had been established. Until that time it was a common belief that only the children of the wealthy families had the opportunity to go to a university. However, with the creation of the preparation center in Manisa and similar institutions in the following years, this common belief started to change. People started to believe that ordinary Turkish families' children could also be placed in universities (Cetin, 2010). Gülen did not take any administrative or teaching position at these institutions. He also did not continue his administrative position at Kestane Pazarı Qur'anic School. However, he continued his lectures until 1991 as an official religious preacher (Erdogan, 1996).

Gülen's lectures, written works, and interviews reveal that he studied and criticized deeply both western and eastern scholars. Such scholars included but were not limited to Mevlana, Sadi, Hafiz, Molla Cami, Firdevsi, and Enveri from the east, as well as Shakespeare, Balzac, Voltaire, Rousseau, Kant, Zola, Goethe, Camus, and Sartre from the west. He also deeply studied and criticized Turkish scholars, poets, thinkers, and novelists including Namik Kemal, Fuzuli, Baki, Seyh Galip, Leyla Hanim, Tevfik Fikret, Mehmet Akif Ersoy, Yahya Kemal, Nurettin Topcu, Cemil Meric and Sezai Karakoc. Concurrent to these efforts, Fethullah Gülen taught advanced Islamic sciences to students beginning during his Edirne years. His classes were in a more traditional form and became more systematic after 1986. Gülen taught and still teaches *Tafsir* (Qur'anic commentary), *Fiqh* (Islamic law), Hadith (Prophet Muhammad's sayings), Sufism, Methodology of Islamic Law, and Grammar (Capan, 2010).

Unal and William (2000) see Gülen as an educator rather than an Islamic preacher. According to them he is an educator not only of the mind but also of the heart and spirit, a description that would form the basis of his reputation. According to Gülen "the main duty and the purpose of human life is to seek understanding. The effort of doing so is known as education" (Unal & Williams, 2000, p. 305). Gülen distinguishes humans from other creatures by emphasizing spiritual and intellectual dimensions. According to him, a human's education continues throughout life. He states that at birth we are wholly impotent and needy. This condition may continue for years unlike other animals. For instance, Gülen states "most animals come into the world as if matured or perfected beforehand. Within a few hours or days or months they learn everything for their survival" (Unal & Williams, 2000, p. 305).

The Gülen Movement

The Gülen Movement is a faith-based socio-cultural movement inspired by the ideas and works of the Turkish scholar and thinker Gülen, whose ideas began to attract adherents in early 1970s. Although he started as an administrator at Kestane Pazarı Islamic School in 1966, it is difficult to say the movement started when he was assigned to the school (Hermansen, 2005). Since Gülen was also assigned to preaching at different mosques in and around Izmir, he found chances to share his thoughts from the mosque pulpits, and continued speeches at coffee houses and at house meetings. His powerful elocution took people's attention and Gülen became a well-known preacher in Izmir. During his Izmir years Gülen also visited several cities in Turkey and gave speeches about diverse subjects (Erdogan, 1996).

The first step of the Gülen Movement's volunteers in forming and educational system in Turkey was opening a university exam preparation center (*dersane*) to prepare students for nationwide university entrance exams that are still extremely competitive. Such *dersanes* became more and more popular since they enjoyed great success, having the champions every single year. Currently the Gülen Movement's *dersanes* are all around the country (Agai, 2005). After a 1980 military coup, the Gülen Movement found opportunities to open state controlled private schools. Gülen encouraged many volunteers to open private schools. With their modern education, those schools used English as their primary language. Like *dersanes*, these schools became well known for their academic success at regional, national and international competitions (Cetin, 2010).

Members of the Gülen Movement started opening schools abroad after the collapse of Soviet Union. The first Gülen-inspired schools outside of Turkey were opened in former Soviet Union countries (e.g., Azerbaijan, Kazakhstan, and Kirgizstan). Like *dersanes* and schools in Turkey, these schools became well known for their successes in a relatively short time period. Accordingly, the Gülen Movement opened schools in other countries (Unal & Williams, 2000). Though the exact number of these schools is not known, they are estimated at more than a thousand schools in over 100 countries (Ebaugh, 2009). Although the educational institutions of the Gülen Movement provide primarily K-12 education, the movement also has universities, dormitories, and language schools in and outside of Turkey.

The Gülen Movement is well known for its school networks in several countries. Yavuz (2004) describes the movement as an education-oriented movement, and emphasizes educational activities as the primary concern of the movement. However, the Gülen Movement also established a newspaper (Zaman) a TV station, (Samanyolu), several radio stations, publishing companies, hospitals (Sema, Sifa), and several magazines (Aksiyon, Sizinti, Yeni Umit) in Turkey. Some of the magazines published in different languages. Another indicator of the success of the Gülen Movement is that the Zaman newspaper has the highest number of daily readers in Turkey (Cetin, 2010).

For a better and more comprehensive understanding of the Gülen Movement, it is essential to look at some of the beliefs and characteristics of the movement that distinguish it from other movements. Aras & Caha define the movement as Islamic, nationalist, liberal and modern, whereas, Yavuz (2003) does not accept Gülen's Islamic approach as liberal; instead he suggests it is pragmatic and contemporary.

Islam as a Driving Force

Fethullah Gülen has a religious background and has used Islamic sources to motivate and mobilize the movement's volunteers since his Kestane Pazari years. In order to better understand the movement's characteristics, it is important to understand Gülen's interpretation of Islam.
According to Yavuz (2004) Gülen represents a new model of Islam
in Turkey. This model briefly is at peace with democracy and modernity. Yavuz (2004) also sees this model as the Anatolian understanding of Islam. On the other hand, other researchers (Kim, 2005; Cetin,
2010) emphasize the Sufi conception of morality as the core value of
the movement. However, as Gokcek (2005) states, Gülen follows the
basic principles' of the Sufi order that do not conflict with the modern world. Further, Kim (2005) defines the movement as "quasi-Su-
fi", or "Sufi-oriented" with respect to the important role of the Sufi tradition in the movement. Williams (2005) defines the Gülen Movement
as a "social movement" rather than as a Sufi denomination.

Sufism, in brief, is the spiritual side of Islam or the inner life of a
practicing Muslim (Chittick, 1999). Luckily we have a definition of
Sufism in Gülen's own words: "Sufism is the path followed by an individual who, having been able to free himself or herself from human
vices and weakness in order to acquire angelic qualities and conduct
pleasing to God, lives in accordance with the requirements of God's
knowledge and love, and in the resulting spiritual delight that ensues."
(Gülen, 1999, p. xiv).

In addition to this definition, Yavuz (2004) indicates that the
major sources of Sufism are the Qur'an and the Sunnah (the tradi-
tions of Prophet Muhammad, peace and blessings be upon him).

Gülen motivates his audiences with Islamic values that are embed-
ded in universal values. He mostly uses examples from Prophet Muhammad and people who lived around him that are named as Sahaba (the
Companions). His historical Islamic examples also include Muslim
leaders and scholars throughout history. Some examples include stories that emphasize how service to humanity is valued by God (Unal
& Williams, 2000). Such stories also included the Qur'an's verses, and
Prophet Muhammad's sayings. For instance, Gülen (2004b) states that

"curing a person who has a disease may be more valuable than 1000 sessions of optional prayer to God" (p. 4). He emphasizes that it was a duty for every Muslim to ease the problems of human beings regardless of their religion, nationality or location on the earth. Although Islam was seen as the driving force to open GIS schools, it must be emphasized that the GIS around the world are operated as secular schools that do not offer religious instruction as a part of their curriculum.

Dialogue

Interfaith dialogue became one of the central activities of the Gülen Movement. Developing understanding through dialogue is also rooted in the volunteers' religious philosophy. Dialogue activities with diverse groups became part of the Gülen Movement's identity (Ebaugh, 2009). Gülen met with different religious leaders including the Pope John Paul II. Volunteers of the Gülen Movement organized activities in Turkey and abroad designed to increase the kind of dialogues that had become a fundamental characteristic of the movement. In his teachings, Gülen (2004a) emphasizes importance of communication and tolerance:

"Among the many things we have lost, perhaps the first and most important is tolerance. From this word we understand embracing people regardless of difference of opinion, world-view, ideology, ethnicity, or belief. It also means putting up with matters we do not like by finding strength in a deep conscience, faith and a generous heart or by strength of our emotions. From another approach, it means, in the words of the famous Turkish poet Yunus, loving the created simply because of the Creator." (p. 46).

Gülen builds a new language with dialogue without sacrificing Islam's basic disciplines. To do so Gülen follows the Qur'an, the Sunnah, and Muslim intellectual's tradition (Aslandogan & Cetin, 2007). Caha and Aras (2000) claim however, that Gülen's approach is not new and comes from the Anatolian people's interpretation and experience of Islam. Parallel to this claim, Gülen emphasizes "Turkish Muslimness" (Ozkok, 1995; Can 1995). In other words, with respect to Islam's universality as most of the religions, Gülen accepts the interpretation of Islam in Anatolia as Turkish Islam.

According to Gülen (2000a), interfaith dialogue seeks to realize religion's basic oneness and unity and the universality of belief. It is not an attempt at creating a new religion or a combination of religions. Furthermore, the purpose of interfaith dialogue is not one of destroying scientific materialism and the materialistic worldview. According to him the nature of religion requires dialogue. Gülen (2000a) emphasizes the accepted values in all religions as tolerance, love, respect, mercy, human rights, freedom, peace and so on. These values are the common points for dialogue among all religions.

On the other hand, Gülen (2000a) also emphasizes his methodology of dialoging with other people. By doing so, he draws the road map for the volunteers for their own attempts at creating dialogue. Gülen (2000a) states:

"Be so tolerant that your heart becomes wide like the ocean. Become inspired with faith and love for others. Offer a hand to those in trouble, and be concerned about everyone... Applaud the good for their goodness, appreciate those who have believing hearts, and be kind to believers. Approach unbelievers so gently that their envy and hatred melt away. Like a Messiah, revive people with your breath." (p. 61).

Gülen's Education Philosophy and the Gülen-Inspired Schools

According to Gülen (2000) there are two main aspects of education. The first aspect of it is at the individual level and the second one is at the community level. Thus, education is the essence of humanity, and sustains a well-balanced society. Michel (2005), who studied various Gülen Inspired schools in different countries, says that Gülen's educational philosophy based on the Turkish experience, where modern secular schools have been unable to free themselves from the prejudices and conventions of modernist ideology. In other words, with his perspective on education, Gülen (1996) envisions the "marriage of hearts and minds," a combination of science, reason, and morality, hoping to form individuals of "thought, action, and inspiration".

Gülen sees education as an effort to seek understanding. Accordingly, he states that "the main duty of human life is a perfecting process through which we earn, in the spiritual, intellectual, and physical dimensions of our beings, the rank appointed for us as the perfect pattern of creation" (Unal & Williams, 2000, p. 305). Furthermore, according to Gülen, education distinguishes human from other creatures: "We are truly human if we learn, teach, and inspire others. It is difficult to regard those who are ignorant and without desire to learn as truly human" (Unal & Williams, 2000, p. 309). According to Unal and Williams (2000), Gülen accepts education as a solution for three major problems of developing countries, poverty, ignorance, and division. These problems can be treated through education.

For a better understanding of Gülen's educational philosophy and Gülen-inspired schools, it is essential to look at the brief history of the Gülen-inspired schools. The first official educational activity of the movement took place in 1978. The Gülen Movement established private university preparatory centers that prepared students university exams that are still very competitive in Turkey. A 1980 military coup provided an opportunity to open private schools for the movement, and the movement started opening private schools near the university preparatory centers. Private Yamanlar High School in Izmir and Private Fatih High School in Istanbul were opened as the movement's first high schools in 1982. The success of those schools and preparatory centers brought the movement's name into the media. In the early 1990s, after the dissolution of the Soviet Union, volunteers of the Gülen Movement opened high quality high schools in former Soviet Union countries, (e.g., Azerbaijan, Kazakhstan and Turkmenistan) and then all over the world. In the following years, with donations from supporters, Gülen inspired civic initiatives, and established hundreds of schools in different countries as named "Gülen-inspired schools" (Aslandogan & Cetin, 2007).

Gülen-inspired schools around the world provide secular education, and are well known with their emphasis on the sciences. Each

school is independently run, but there is a shared vision for the curriculum, (Williams, 2005), which is shaped by local and international
requirements. Michel (2005, p. 3) states that "Gülen-inspired schools
have universal Islamic values such as honesty, hard work, harmony,
and conscientious service rather than any confessional instructions".
According to Cetin (2010) the Gülen Movement believes that we live
in a global world, Muslims, non-Muslims, and all different ethnic groups
live in the same community, therefore we have to create a shared understanding, a shared experience, and a shared code of ethics. According
to Yavuz (2004), the Gülen Movement tries to accomplish this through
education, and that is the reason that they opened schools in China,
in Russia, and in Africa. All kinds of teachers are employed in these
schools: Turkish, non-Turkish, Muslim, and non-Muslim. According
to Agai (2005) in many cases students have never heard the name of
Fethullah Gülen; in that sense it may be inaccurate to call these schools
Gülen schools, on the other hand, Gülen inspired the establishment of
these schools and without his efforts these schools would have never
existed.

Because of their academic success but also their ability to operate
in diverse cultures, these schools have attracted both academic and
media attention. While *The New York Times* suggests Gülen-inspired
schools in Pakistan could be a remedy to radical interpretations of Islam
(Tavernise, 2008), *Le Monde* offers these schools as good examples compared to Europe's low performing minorities (Borne, 2008). Thomas
Michel (Michel, 2005), former Ecumenical Secretary at the Asias Desk
of the Vatican Pontifical Council for Interreligious Dialogue, states that
these schools have reached millions of children all across the world and
helped with their education regardless of their race, language, religion
or nationality.

Several scholars studied Gülen-inspired schools in different countries (Agai, 2005, Michel, 2005, Ozdalga 2005, Akyol, 2008, Irvine,
2007, Kalyoncu, 2008). Agai (2005), who investigated Gülen-inspired
schools in Albania, focused on the contribution of the schools to the
community which had been governed by a communist system for
decades. He emphasized the contributions of the schools in the forms

of their humanitarian accomplishments. According to Agai (2005), Gülen's religious values are reflected as a language of ethics and in the form of dialogue. The schools' moral qualities were highly appreciated by the parents of students. Furthermore the technical skills and the success of the schools were well known not only in Albania but also in the international arena. On the other hand Michel (2005) investigated schools in the Philippines, Kirgizstan, Turkey, and many other countries. in accordance with Agai (2005), Michel (2005) states that these schools were well known for their academic success in both national and international areas. Furthermore the schools' contributions to the community in terms of ethical and humanitarian efforts were also emphasized. For instance, in Philippines a Gülen-inspired school named "The Filipino-Turkish School of Tolerance" was located in Zamboanga that had a 50%Muslim and 50% Christian population. Zamboanga was struggling with guerilla warfare with frequent kidnappings, disappearances, and arrests. In this city, the school offered education for both Muslim and Christian Filipino children. Michel emphasizes that the school while providing an excellent education was also promoting and teaching tolerance to both Muslim and Christian students and greatly contributed to the needs of the community. The school was supported by local groups and had a good reputation.

One of the most important characteristics of these schools was their ability to adapt to the new cultures and educational systems of diverse countries. Opening noticeably successful schools in a relatively short time, in more than 100 countries in different cultures and educational systems attracted the attention not only of scholars but also of politicians and educators seeking new strategies and applicable policies for the young generations.

Aslandogan and Cetin (2007) state that the successes of these schools comes from Gülen's educational philosophy which has four dimensions. Paradigm shift is the first dimension and it is explained as "a new appreciation for the enterprise of education and profession of teaching, elevating both to noble status" (p. 31). In other words Gülen sees teachers who represent the universal values as the primary driving force of the educational activism which is also the primary solution for the current socio-economic problems of society. Gülen (2004) also points out the characteristics of good teachers: "Real teachers...occupy themselves with what is good and wholesome and lead and guide the children in life and whatever events encounter...In addition to setting good personal example, teachers should be patient enough to obtain the desired result. They should know their students very well, and address their intellects and their hearts, sprit and feelings" (p. 208).

According to Aslandogan and Cetin (2007), the second dimension of Gülen's educational philosophy centers around altruism and dedication, which require eliminating selfishness and establishing the spirit of community service in the field of education. Gülen accepted altruism as a key concept to convince people who sponsor teducational projects. Furthermore, Gülen's message to teachers and prospective teachers includes this key concept. Gülen emphasizes the purpose of human creation as serving fellow citizens and humanity. Probably the most effective example of this key concept is Gülen's own altruism. Gülen has a very modest background, does not have worldly wealth, and does not have any direct connection to any schools that are founded by volunteers, and further, Gülen has no financial linkages with GIS schools. These facts also contribute to the trust and assurance in Gülen's own altruism among the volunteers that follow his philosophy. Gülen's altruistic philosophy is best expressed in his own words:

"I grew up with the desire and objective to serve my country... I have never thought of having house, children, or a car. You can not oppose natural laws: water flows, condenses at 100 Celsius, and freezes at 0 Celsius. If there is such characteristics in my nature, if it is not harmful what could be more natural than for this seed to flourish?" (Unal & Williams, 2000, p. 326)

The third dimension of Gülen's educational philosophy is the epistemological dimension. According to Aslandogan and Cetin (2007), this third dimension explains "the synthesis of the mind and the heart, the traditional and the modern, the spiritual and intellectual" (p. 32). In other words, Gülen (2000a) proposes a middle way among radical approaches that generally seem to clash. For instance, science and religion have been seen contradictory to each other in many cases. Gülen offers his middle way that reconciles science and religion both in theory and in practice. The middle way achieves a harmony of reason and faith:

"Avoiding the positive sciences out of fear that they will lead to atheism is childishness, and seeing them as opposed to religion and faith and as vehicle for the rejection of religion is prejudice and ignorance...One who profoundly thinks about and evaluates nature and the laws of life will see the coquetry of eternal beauty in everything, and hear the consecration of infinite power in every sound - from flowers' shining colors to swaying tree branches, from frightening thunderclaps to sparrows' harmonious songs. Such people see the traces and works of a divine sources manifested in the phenomena and laws such as light and heat, attraction and chemical reaction, and the direction of animate beings." (Gülen, 2000a, p. 42).

The last dimension of Gülen's educational philosophy is cooperation among educators, parents, and sponsors which can be interpreted as the social dimension. For this dimension, Aslandogan and Cetin (2007) point out societies' expectations from education as "every society looks for education for their children that does not conflict with their cultural heritage and values" (p. 44). According to Aslandogan and Cetin (2007), Gülen's educational approach, while accepting and applying modern methods and curriculum, was not in conflict with tradition and the culture of society. In other words, Gülen-inspired schools endow modern education excelling in math, science, language, arts and sports while retaining the common moral values. This peace between cultural heritage and modern education attracted the attention of parents and sponsors. Schools became more attractive by their success within a short time period. Furthermore schools supported poor families' children who cannot attend private school because of financial difficulties. The sponsors realized that they were paying for the education of not only their own children but also additional economically disadvantaged students as well. Some parents and sponsors took extra steps to establish scholarship for thousands of students. Furthermore altruism that is reflected on teachers who exemplified the importance of being law-abiding and living with moral accountability was also effective in attracting the attention of sponsors and parents, and earned their trust for their children's education.

According to Aslandogan and Cetin, (2007) there are three major factors that make Gülen-inspired schools attractive for parents and educational systems around the world:

1) A satisfactory combination of tradition and modernity including science, reason, and technology, and proven academic achievement in these fields.

2) The altruistic approach of the well-qualified and well-trained teachers and educators, and the lack of profit-seeking.

3) Non-politicization of educational, scientific, and cultural issues, as well as their institutions and efforts (p. 47).

Social Capital

Cohen and Prusak (2001) define social capital as "the stock of active connections among people; the (a) trust, (b) mutual understanding, and (c) shared values and behaviors that bind the members of human networks and communities and make cooperative action possible" (p. 4). Emphasizing the role and function of social capital, Cohen and Prusak examine how social capital works in organizations, how social capital investments are made, and the return on social capital investments that is enjoyed by organizations and individuals (p. 3). According to Cohen and Prusak (2001), the generation and access of social capital is a dynamic, organic process.

Coleman (1988) illustrates the role of social capital in society with his story of the family of eight who immigrated from suburban Detroit to Jerusalem in order to gain greater freedom of movement. The mother of this family felt that unsupervised play in a city park in Jerusalem would be safe for her six children. She would also feel safe allowing her eight-year-old daughter to take a younger sibling to school across town on the city bus. According to Coleman, the difference between Jerusalem and suburban Detroit is a difference in social capital. Unlike most metropolitan regions in the United States, the normative structure of Jerusalem provides social capital such that unattended children will be "looked after" by adults. In short, this mother believed she would be more comfortable living in Jerusalem because there was more social capital available to her family there (Coleman 1988).

Aslandogan and Cetin (2007) assert that in an educational context, social capital is generated when educator-parent-sponsorship (community) relationships are established and triangulated. Social capital results from parental involvement and non-parental involvement alike. Aslandogan and Cetin (2007) also emphasize that one of the most important dimensions of Gülen's educational philosophy is establishing these educator-parent-sponsorship (community) relationships and networking. They note that establishing social capital among stakeholders is critical. Variations in the success of an entire school or an individual student can be attributed to the differing levels of existing social capital generated by a school's community network and families. A school that is disciplined and that emphasizes academics will generate social capital that supports educational success, as will a society whose values and cultural norms motivate students to achieve higher goals.

Many researchers (Bankston, 2004; Field, 2003; Horvat, et al., 2003) emphasize the importance of social capital in education. They recognize that manifestations of social capital can be observed in educational settings, and so it is common to see examples from the field of education used in examinations of social capital. Comparative studies are made of social capital in different educational systems (e.g., two cultures grounded in disparate philosophies), and social capital theory can also be applied when addressing current educational problems in order to identify alternative, applicable educational philosophies and practices (Acar, 2011).

CHAPTER 3

Methodology

Research Design

The purpose of this case study was to describe the characteristics of one Gülen-inspired school (GIS) in the United States. This study identified the characteristics of a U.S. based GIS in terms of the school's curriculum, history, success, hiring process, admission process and networking. The researcher designed a qualitative case study since qualitative method tolerates more flexibility and openness to contextual interpretation. This methodology allows researchers to conduct an inquiry that seeks to understand social contexts according to participants' perspectives (Merriam & Associates, 2002). Yin (2003) states that a case study design should be considered when: (a) the key point of the study is answering "how" and "why"; (b) the researcher does not affect the behaviors of participants; and (c) the center of attention is related to the real life experiences. According to Yin (2003), such characteristics distinguish case studies from other designs. Further, case study designs do not have carefully delineated boundaries compared to other qualitative designs. Yin (2003) also adds that case studies are the most challenging designs, especially for social science researchers.

According to Yin (2003) case study designs are commonly used to study specific social concepts with the inquiry of individuals, groups or organizations. These types of case studies are used in the examination of real life interactions by researchers who hope to explain assumed causal links. This approach is used when the complexity of real life interactions preclude the use of surveys or of experimental methodologies. Consequently, case studies are a common research method in psychology, sociology, political science, social work, business, nursing and education (Yin, 2003).

Data Collection Procedure

For this case study, the research question was stated as follows: "How is the philosophy of a "Gülen-inspired school" reflected in a United States based GIS, as it relates to its curriculum, history, success, hiring process, admission process and networking? " The researcher first submitted a study proposal to the Marywood University's Institutional Review Board. Following approval, (See Appendix A) the researcher contacted the principal of GIS to present details about the potential study following which the principal's approval for the study was received by the researcher.

For the administrators' interviews the researcher prepared a consent form (See Appendix B) and twelve interview questions (See Appendix C). After the completion of the consent form the principal of the school was interviewed. The guidance counselor of the school who was also the vice principal of the school was then interviewed. Each interview was completed in a two hour session in the principal's office.

For the teachers' interviews, the researcher contacted potential interviewees during the first observation session at GIS. Six teachers were available and willing to participate in the study. Those teachers completed a consent form (See Appendix D). The researcher asked the teachers six interview questions (See Appendix E). The interviewed teachers represented 25% of the teacher population at GIS. Each teacher interview was completed in a one hour session outside the school (e.g., coffee houses, restaurants, etc).

The researcher also contacted several parents during the first observation session at GIS. Six parents who were available and willing to participate in the study completed a consent form (See Appendix F). The researcher asked parents six interview questions (See Appendix G). Each parent interview was also completed in a one hour session at different locations (e.g., coffee houses, restaurants) with respect to the parents' preferences.

All of the interviews were tape recorded by the researcher and transcribed verbatim by a professional transcriber. Further, for validation purposes, the researcher sent transcribed verbatim interviews to all interviewed people for their approval. The interview transcriptions provided a natural inquiry comprising the interviewees' feelings, opinions, experiences and beliefs, as manifested in direct quotations (Patton, 1990). Furthermore, beside the interviews, the researcher observed class sessions, extra curricula sessions, interactions among teachers, students, parents and administrators, activities that also included parents and community members. Observations were conducted during the school year and completed over a period of four months. The researcher used a notebook to record his observations.

A review of pertinent school documents including report cards, transcripts, attendance letters, disciple notices, teacher certifications, and sports performances was also conducted during the study. The researcher was allowed to review these documents in order to augment and support the interviews and observations made by the participating family and faculty of the GIS.

In order to describe and reveal themes, the researcher read the transcribed interviews several times. During the reading of interview transcriptions, the researcher took notes in the margins of the transcriptions. The notes included repeated common ideas and words. Then the researcher prepared a list of potential themes drawn from the observation notes and pertinent documents. Subsequently, the researcher carefully analyzed and compared the emergent themes and it was apparent that four emerged as promoting an understanding of the "underlying meaning" (Creswell, 2003, p. 155) of the GIS under study.

Table 1: *Frequency Distribution for Gender of Participants*

Stakeholders	Total number of Participants	Gender (M/F)	Sample Pool (%)
Teachers	6	4/2	42.8
Parents	6	4/2	42.8
Administrators	2	2/0	14.2
Total	14	10/4	100

Table 2: *Frequency Distribution of the Age of Participants*

Stakeholders	Age Distribution	Total Number	Sample Pool (%)
Teachers	23-33	6	42.8
Parents	32-56	6	42.8
Administrators Average	30-38 35.3	2 -	14.2 -
Total	-	14	100

Table 3: *Teaching/Administrative Experience of GIS's interviewed personnel*

Stakeholders	Years of Experience in Education (Average)	Years of Experience in Education at GIS (Average)
GIS's all teachers GSI's all administrators	8.5 8	4.5 4

Study Instruments

The researcher conducted categorized open-ended interviews with school personnel and parents. Interview questions were designed with respect to the research question of the study. According to Creswell (2003), open-ended questions allow the participants to form opinions for answering questions. The number of questions varied according to the position and the role of individuals in the school.

It was the researcher's belief that information gained from the administrators would provide insight into the true philosophy of the school. In other words, GIS's administrators would present valuable information about the school's history, personnel, curricula, success, activities, and networks with other stakeholders. In addition to the questions for background information, school administrators received twelve open-ended questions (See Appendix C). Further, in order to gain information about teaching strategies, lesson plans, extra curricula activities, relationships with students, parents and community members, the researcher prepared six open-ended interview questions for the teachers in addition to the background information questions (See

Appendix E). On the other hand, since parents, in one perspective, are the primary stakeholders of their children's education and have the highest responsibility, it was expected that the researcher would learn valuable information about the school from their viewpoint. Accordingly the researcher prepared six open-ended interview questions for the parents excluding the background information questions (See Appendix G).

Conclusion

With specific interview questions, the researcher expected to reveal all the aspects of Gülen's educational philosophy that are reflected in the practices and policies of the GIS. The researcher also expected to find specific characteristics of the school with respect to the culture or uniqueness of the region where the school is located.

CHAPTER 4

Findings

E ducational practices reflect different philosophies. Although governments set general rules and regulations for education systems to promote standardization, the application of different types of educational philosophies is allowed since there is no consensus on the most effective educational philosophy and model. The purpose of this case study was to describe a Gülen-inspired school (GIS) in the United States. This study identified the characteristics of a U.S. based GIS, including the school's curriculum, history, academic success, hiring process, admission process and networking. Accordingly, the study tried to answer the research question of "How is the philosophy of a "Gülen-inspired school" reflected in a United States based GIS, as it relates to curriculum, history, success, hiring process, admission process and networking?" This study identifies unique characteristics of a U.S. based GIS with respect to Gülen's educational philosophy.

To describe the GIS, the study presents the results of the analysis of qualitative data collected from participants who are affiliated with the GIS through individual interviews, observations and pertinent GIS documents. For the study, fourteen participants from three stakeholder categories (administrators, teachers, and parents) were interviewed in the spring of 2011. This chapter presents the data collected in the interviews, observations, and review of pertinent GIS documents.

Four themes emerged from the analyzed qualitative data:
1. A strong emphasis on quality science education.
2. The school personnel's altruism and dedication to teaching.
3. A safe school environment.

4. A strong sense of school, family and community relationship values.

A Strong Emphasis on Quality Science Education

It was apparent that the school curriculum placed great emphasis on education in the sciences. Interviewed school administrators and teachers, regardless of discipline, frequently mentioned the school's emphasis on science education. Further, all six interviewed parents were aware of the school's science-oriented curriculum. However, as the interviewed school administrators indicated, social science courses were also offered as a part of the educational program at the GIS. Interviewed school administrators were comfortable with the school's reputation as a science-oriented school in the region. When asked about science-oriented education, the principal of the GIS presented his view:

> [GIS] focuses on science and math education, and also engineering, so our curriculum is a little bit different from other public schools. I can say that our school is [a] science-oriented school, but in our curriculum we have all the subjects: history, social sciences, and languages.

Several scholars (Mehmeti, 2009; Santos 2006; Woodhall, 2005) indicate that Gülen-inspired schools around the world focus on science education. In this instance, the GIS can be defined as a science-oriented school since several indicators prove that there is a significant emphasis on science education in the curriculum. The emphasis on science education was mentioned frequently by the school personnel. The principal of the school also said the following:

"We are offering more science and math courses. Regular schools offer, [at] maximum, six hours [of] math and science courses in middle schools. We are giving eight hours math and science courses, and also in high school we offer more science elective courses, e.g. AP Biology, AP Physics and AP Chemistry. We strongly recommend our students to take AP exams…Also, some scientific and math competition programs are in our curriculum."

Interviewed vice principal offered his view:

"Actually, I cannot say that there is much difference when you compare our curriculum with other schools, but what we ask our teachers is that there will be modifications to the curriculum, especially in science and math subjects. Especially in the high school, we are offering many AP and elective science courses."

Furthermore, scholastic achievement at the school showed that the real focus of the school's curriculum was around science and math education. Most of the medals from national and international competitions came from science-oriented contests. Discussing student awards, interviewed vice principal said the following:

"When you look at the history of our school, we have many medals in science and mathematics competitions. We got 32 gold medals, and this shows that in our school science and math subjects are taught very carefully and they are taught in advance. We hire very experienced teachers who are dedicated to their job. I think this is also one of the differences when comparing our school with other schools. Our parents know that if they send their kids to our school that they will learn the science subjects, like chemistry physics, and mathematics very well."

In the spring of 2011, when this case study was conducted, GIS received several medals from national science competitions. At a state-level robotics competition, GIS's team received the judge's special award. Further, at a state-level math contest held at Princeton University, GIS took second place. At a state-level computer contest, GIS also took second place. Lastly, at the Science Olympiads held at the New Jersey Institute of Technology, GIS received one silver and three bronze medals.

Central to the GIS emphasis on curriculum are the modifications made by administrators and teachers to improve the academic success of students. The school allowed and encouraged teachers to design and modify their curriculum with minor changes for better effectiveness. All interviewed teachers indicated that they were making necessary changes for better academic success. Teachers were preparing their own syllabi to meet general requirements. However, all interviewed teachers indicated that they were preparing modifications as a team. In other words, teachers who were teaching the same subjects were finalizing their individual syllabi with their colleagues. One interviewed teacher said the following:

"We have adapted some curriculum from the public district, and we modify it according to our needs. Since this is a private school we are not bound by state standards, but we cover all the state's standards and we try to go beyond."

An interviewed computer science teacher offered his thoughts:

"If you are a computer science teacher, you are on your own. There is no computer science curriculum in the US. Every state has something different and they don't have printed books. They don't have a workshop about it. So, if you look at the public schools around here, they don't really have a computer science department in their schools. Most of the schools, including public schools around here, when they talk about computer science they just teach some basic computer skills, not computer science exactly. So, what we are doing here is that we are trying to draw a curriculum close to universities, like AP courses for computer science."

An interviewed math teacher said the following:

"I teach math. I am not only using one text book but also using several additional books to modify my syllabus. I also do not stick with what I prepared at the beginning of the semester. I leave some blank spots in the syllabus and fill them with respect to the students' educational progress during the semester. If even this is not enough for the needs of students, I schedule extra class hours after the regular class schedules. We are very flexible when we design our syllabuses. But that does not mean that we teach whatever we would like to teach."

Both administrators and the interviewed teachers pointed out that students from all grades are not only prepared for the following year but also for the college entrance exams and for college courses. Especially when a student starts high school at GIS, the real focus of the curriculum was college entrance exams (i.e. SAT, ACT). Further, they try to design curriculums that take students' future college needs into account according to the principal of the GIS:

"Especially the AP courses are designed for students' future needs in college courses. We want our students to be ready for the university. We believe that they have this much learning capacity in the high school. They learn here and they become more comfortable at the college. They take fewer courses at college. I mean they receive exemption and they pay less."

The vice principal of GIS said agreed:

"We are preparing our students for the colleges. And naturally, the first step is preparing students for the college entrance exams. Especially the tutoring sessions are very important for this preparation. Each student requires special care since each student has own plans for the future. Different interests require one-on-one care."

It was easily noticeable that the curricula of the GIS were designed with respect to the future college life of the students. An interviewed biology teacher emphasized the importance of AP courses for the students' college experience in the future:

"AP courses are advanced placement courses and when students take those courses they learn a lot of information about the content area, and then at the end of the year they take the AP biology test, which is like [the] SAT test, and then if they pass that exam, they get exemption about 9-10 credits. Of course it depends on the college and the major. It changes, but they get credits from the colleges."

Another indicator of the emphasis on curriculum was the use of after-class scheduling to meet students' needs. Observations supported that teachers of GIS covered course subjects in greater detail during the tutoring sessions. Additional course subject details were also provided to students who participate in science Olympiads and science fair competitions. Honors classes also received more detailed curriculum instruction at the GIS. One interviewed teacher explained it this way:

"We also try to help them with their college entrance tests, like SAT's/ACT's. Whenever a student needs help with those tests, we study with them after school or on weekends and go into more detail in those subjects. Also, in our honors classes, we teach the subject with more detail. Also, we try to challenge our talented students with competitions. We participate in science Olympiad and science fair competitions, and we work with our students to prepare them for those events. Also, if a student needs help we work with them one-on-one after school."

Both school administrators also pointed out the school's science laboratories, which are equipped with the latest technology. There was one biology laboratory, one chemistry laboratory, and one computer laboratory at GIS. The biology laboratory has also been used for earth and physical science courses. The vice principal also indicated that they were using smart boards in all classrooms. Interviewed science teachers emphasized that they were very comfortable using the latest technology at the school's laboratories. An interviewed biology teacher said the following:

"We have a biology lab that has everything we need. Whatever we request from the administrators, they provide. You know that without a lab or with a lack of equipment, teachers cannot teach and students cannot learn well. Biology is not only about theory. Students need to see real experiments, and we have the ability to show them in our labs. Let me give you some examples. We do DNA extraction and fingerprinting in our labs. We are able to do animal and plant dissection in order to show anatomy. We also go for field work for better understanding of ecology and vegetation."

An interviewed chemistry teacher also responded that "science cannot be taught without experiments and practices. Students see real science. I mean that science in action."

The social science curriculum at the GIS, including history, geography, American government, and language education, was similar to the curriculum offered in public schools. Both interviewed administrators said that the social science curriculum is also modified and improved for the needs of students at GIS. Student SAT scores and a clear student preference for choosing science majors in college show that science education at the GIS has the priority. Further, compared to science contests, national and international medals that came from social science competitions were fewer in number. However, it cannot be claimed that the school downgraded the social science education of their students, according to the principal of the GIS:

"Although the real emphasis on curriculum goes to science education, we try to keep the balance between social science and science education. Let's say it this way: We are good with the social science education, but really good with science education. You know what I mean."

According to the interviewed social science teacher:

"We are doing less modification on the social science curriculum. The reason is simple: because it is social science. You cannot change the history, and this is not limited to history classes. But you can look at the history from different angles. Imagine that World War II is the subject in the history class, and teaching facts of it…like the names, dates, key battles, is very easy. However, teaching the subject with respect to the effects and causes of it makes the difference. Teaching this subject with regards to the current world realities is the effective teaching. We do that here at [GIS]. "

Although the focus has been on science, the interviewed vice principal explained that "people may think that we are only teaching science courses. The reason is that we have the reputation in science competitions. There are fewer competitions in social sciences."

The interviews also revealed that all interviewed parents were highly aware of the school's emphasis on science education. All six parents who were interviewed knew that the school is a science-oriented school. However, none of the interviewed parents said that they sent their children to the GIS solely because of the strong science education curriculum. Half of the interviewed parents said that their children attended science-oriented clubs and they were very happy since their students were selected for the competitions. One interviewed parent said the following:

"There is an emphasis on science education and math education. It is true that science and math education is very good in the school. They have skilled teachers doing the science and math education, but they don't neglect the social studies, art and music classes. So, your kid takes and gets a balanced educational program in the school."

Another interviewed parent answered in support of the emphasis on quality education:

"I chose this school because of the education. I see a real, effective education here. Students graduate from this school and go to colleges. The school has high graduation and university placement rates.

Especially the science education is good here. There are several competitions, and the kids at the school are participating in those organizations. And they receive medals."

A typical response from interviewed parents follows:

"There are other schools in this area. I choose this school since I like the education here. I mean kids are learning well here. The curriculum is well-designed. Every student goes to college after graduation. I hear that they do really good at the colleges. One of my friends, whose child graduated from [GIS], said to me that his kid received exemption from some math courses since he had very good math background. I mean, at [GIS] some courses are beyond the high school level."

The principal of the school stated that their curriculum is very effective and brought success to the school. He indicated how the teachers and administrators inform parents about the curriculum at GIS, including the activities that they organize:

"I believe it's effective because it's tailored by our teachers. And with this curriculum we have success stories at different competitions. In addition, the graduation rate is 100%, and all of the GIS graduates are enrolled in four-year colleges. On the other hand, we believe that parents need to know what is being taught here. We try to explain what our curriculum is about when we get chances. Like at PTO meetings. We believe that if they know how their kids are taken care of here, we get better parental involvement and, accordingly, better academic and disciplinary success for the school."

All interviewed administrators, teachers and parents gave strong testimony to the academic success of the school and the quality of its programs.

School Personnel's Altruism and Dedication to Teaching

Aslandogan and Cetin (2007) state that two of the most important principles of Gülen's educational philosophy are altruism and dedication to teaching. Aslandogan and Cetin (2007) also state that Gülen's message to teachers and prospective teachers is simple. The purpose of a human being's creation is to serve fellow citizens and humanity through education. Gülen recognized teachers as the key builders of the future, and their devotion was the spirit of these future builders. According to Ergene (2006, p. 330), Gülen's broader concept of "teacher" also included key stakeholders in the society, such as parents, philosophers, and government administrators. According to Gülen (2004a), there was a teacher behind every great person in history:

"Today, a transcending responsibility that falls on our shoulders is to rekindle the altruistic desire to let others live in the hearts of our fellow citizens...In such an activism, there is a need to identify a set of shared values that will form the trajectory of such a broad social action which will include all segments of the society, the villager and the city dweller, the intellectual as well as the teacher, the lay person as well as the preacher." (Gülen in Ergene, 2006, p. 330).

The data analysis also showed that Gülen's strong emphasis on altruism and devotion to teaching reveals itself as the second theme at GIS's. Interviews and observations showed that an altruistic world-view is strongly reflected in the school's personnel. There were several indicators that supported the notion of devotion at the GIS. All interviewed administrators and teachers expressed their own devotion to teaching with different phrases. Further, all interviewed parents mentioned the teachers' devotion to education at the GIS. The principal of the GIS corroborated the parents' recognition of devotion to education:

"I think that the main difference of Gülen-inspired schools from other schools is the working process of our teachers. I worked as an administrator and as a teacher in those schools. When I look back, I see that when I was working as a teacher, and I see myself and my friends, my colleagues...we were not working only for the salary. I better say that the salary was not the priority. We were working extra hours. We were giving our students many tutoring sessions. We were doing it just to help our students, just to improve the level of our students and the level of our schools."

The interviewed administrator stressed that devotion is expected from the teachers. The interviewed administrators also indicated that devotion was one of the criteria for hiring and evaluating teachers at the GIS, and the principal expressed the same:

"I worked in a Gülen school as a principal and I hired teachers. The first thing which I tell to the teachers [is] that we don't want teachers who work here and leave the school as soon as the bell rings, without looking back. We don't want that kind of teacher here because if the teacher is not working by heart, they can't make the difference for the school. We don't think that these kinds of teachers will help the students to improve their levels, and when we look at our students, our parents, we see that this devotion makes a difference."

Parallel to this statement, devotion and altruistic approach to teaching were also mentioned by the vice principal. According to the vice principal, "the first requirement of being a [faculty] member at GIS is to sacrifice your time and financial expectations, because you are focusing more on education of kids, not your own interests."

All interviewed teachers emphasized that they shared a similar faith that the success of the school comes from the personnel's devotion to education. Further, all interviewed teachers believed that this is the most important condition that differentiates the GIS from the other schools in the region. One interviewed teacher stated how he sees his job at the GIS:

"As a teacher at [GIS], I really don't take it as being an employee. It is like coming here doing something for what you believe in. It's not like an employee, and there is no such relationship. I can say it's like a family here. You wouldn't call yourself as an employee when you do something in your family—for your family—so this is the first thing I would say."

Another interviewed teacher described the teaching profession this way:

"Teaching is a different job. Success comes from the dedication. This is what I believe. And it is not about teaching biology or math to those kids. Teaching and creating good citizens, who act responsibly, respect others, and believe in democracy. Without dedication there is no such real success."

Another interviewed teacher emphasized that he had different job opportunities after his college graduation, including a family-run business with a high income, but he chose to be a teacher at the GIS. He said he made this decision since he saw teaching as a noble occupation:

"I have graduated from an Ivy League college in the U.S. I have studied engineering and normally would look for a job parallel to my diploma. My family also wanted me to start working in our family business and become the director within a couple of years. But I chose to be a teacher. An engineer or a businessman cannot build the future, but a teacher can. This is what I believe."

When asked his opinion on teaching at GIS, one interviewed teacher said that "we [teachers] are the architects of the future. It is good to know that my students will be good citizens in the future of our society."

All interviewed teachers and parents indicated that the entire staff cares about the students and put the interests of the students before their own. This attitude has been highly appreciated by all interviewed parents, who witness that the teachers work long hours and stay after the end of the school day. All parents in the study acknowledged the teachers' dedication to their children's education. Observations also supported this characteristic of the school's personnel. For instance, teachers served by providing tutoring services after school without charging and by spending their own money on gifts and food for students. All interviewed parents were clearly aware of teachers' dedication and willingness to give. They gave different examples to prove their thoughts about the school personnel's dedication to education. Two interviewed parents said that they know that teachers stay after school hours school for tutoring or club activities for their students' success. Three other interviewed parents highlighted that teachers were treating their children like they were their brothers and sisters. One parent said:

"Teachers won't let any student fall behind. There is a big grant called "No Child Left Behind" and this school is really doing that without a grant; that's the interesting part. I think this is the educational philosophy of the school; the teachers and administrators do not let any student go without learning any particular subject."

Quotes from several parents reinforced the professional commitment of teachers:

"They really want to graduate our kids as good citizens for society. They are highly motivated and they really like their noble job. This is unique. This is the atmosphere of this school. They treat [the students] like they are their brothers and sisters. Students love them. And this is essential to teach something to someone."

"My child really loves this school. And the reason for that is his teachers who really love their jobs. They always care about him. I think the best advantage of teachers is their age. I mean that they are young. They are around their thirties. They are not so old and they get a close relationship with the kids at the school. They play soccer and basketball together. They are like a family and this way students like them and the school. And the success comes. I do not mean the academic success only but also the success of creating good and responsible citizens for the society."

Interviewed parents also highlighted that the schools' policy encouraged personnel to make home visits for their students' success. As the principal of the GIS noted, all school teachers were assigned family visits before and during the educational year. Family visits were designed to allow personnel to get to know their students' home environments and to create better communication with the parents. The principal of the GIS said the following:

"Family visits are in our school policy. All teachers are required to visit all of the parents of their students to see the students' learning environment at home and also to give some suggestions to the parents on how they can help their students to learn better at home. How they can help for the homework and assignments. Furthermore, we try to make a schedule for playing time, internet time and TV time. I believe that during these parent visits we build strong relationships with our parents."

All interviewed teachers themselves indicated that they were visiting their students' homes on a regular basis. These family visits were also perceived by the interviewed parents as evidence of the school personnel's dedication to education. Teacher to student ratio at the GIS was making those visits more pertinent.

All interviewed parents also expressed their appreciation of the teachers' dedication to their students' success as evidenced by these family visits. All interviewed parents said that the family visit policy is unique to GIS and that the visits were demonstrative of the school personnel's dedication to education and their altruistic approach. One parent said the following:

"My child's math teacher came to my home and discussed my child's progress at the school with me and with my wife in front of my kid, and we talked [about] what we all can do more for our child, and we sat together and we decided what has to be done at home. So this is very unique...education continues at home not only at school. Teachers come and they really write something...personal improvement plan, which is called "PIP" at home. So, they put how many minutes my son should watch TV, how many minutes he should play with his "play station", how many minutes he should read every night; everything is set up in those family meetings. So that is very unique and that's the philosophy at the GIS."

The principal noted that the school was also encouraging families to meet in settings outside of their homes. Teachers invited families to their own houses, or to other places (e.g. a restaurant, or a coffee house) to talk about their students. When visiting the family of a student, teachers were even bringing that student's classmates along with them. One interviewed teacher said:

"We form a group of teachers and visit the families and talk to them about their children. That makes them happy. They feel that we are more involved in their kids' lives. We do a lot more things, like we take a group of kids, let's say the students who are members of the Math Counts competition team. We get together and go and have dinner at one of the parent's houses. They see us motivated as a team and working well, so that also helps for better relationships between parents and the school. It also encourages parents to be more involved their children's educational progress."

All interviewed parents also indicated that school personnel were very accessible, and that whenever they wanted to contact school personnel, they could easily make the necessary arrangements. Two interviewed parents compared this accessibility issue with other schools, especially the public ones. All interviewed parents also perceived easy accessibility as an indication of the school personnel's dedication to teaching. One interviewed parent expressed his experience:

"It sometimes takes forever to reach a principal in the public school system, but in our school I call the principal and reach him. If he is busy, I leave a message and he calls me back. I feel very comfortable when I call him. There's no problem. Because I know that they understand my concerns as a parent. I know that my concerns are not ignored by them."

Another interviewed parent said the following:

"They are always available there to talk. Whenever you have a question you can go to their office or to the classroom and you can talk about anything related to your kid. They are open to suggestions, questions, any concerns you might have. So this openness makes you very comfortable relating yourself with the school, you feel you are part of the school; you are not a parent standing on the side and waiting for solutions."

Observations at GIS also supported the principal's assertion that the teachers were working altruistically. Teachers often stay at the school for tutoring sessions and for meetings with parents after regular class hours. Some of the meetings took place informally. Parents occasionally visit without an appointment and to talk to the teachers. The researcher frequently noticed these informal meetings.

Many teachers also remained at the school for tutoring sessions after the regular class hours. One interviewed teacher said:

"We stay at the school for tutoring sessions after classes. We are not paid for those extra hours. This is how we think about the education of our students. I mean if a student needs extra care, we help him until he learns whatever subject he was not good at. Education has the priority here. Some teachers might think different but to me money comes after the education."

Another interviewed teacher reinforced the dedication of the GIS teachers:

"Tutoring sessions are very helpful for students' academic achievements. Some students were not learning well in a class environment. And we do not want to leave any student behind. But I have to say that teachers are sacrificing their time here, and do not complain. Administrators are expecting them to stay at the school for tutoring, but there is no written policy for those tutoring sessions."

A final example of the teachers' devotion and altruistic approach to education can be found in the consistent cooperation that teachers exercise in order to meet the school's needs. At GIS, there was strong cooperation among teachers. For instance, all interviewed teachers indicated their willingness to be a part of the preparation of any kind of activity being organized at the GIS. One interviewed teacher said: "We always help each other out. We always try to come together and talk about what we can do to make [a] better learning environment for our students. It's like a family relationship." Observations were especially supportive of identification of this characteristic of the GIS teachers.

An interviewed social science teacher said the following:

"We are like a family here, and every family wants their children to be well educated and well behaved in the society. We [teachers] work in harmony here. We always support each other. We have good communication and cooperation. If something [is] beneficial for the students, we all work together as a team. For example, we organize science fairs at our school, and I am on the team for the preparation of the program."

The principal of the GIS confirmed the collaborative spirit among the faculty. He acknowledged a strong spirit of camaraderie.

Additionally, the curriculum in the GIS does not include religious instruction of any nature. The GIS is not attached to a mosque, church or temple. The vice principal of the GIS stated the following:

"I received a call today from a prospective parent. She said that she and her husband are police officers in the town and they are looking for a secular private school and she called us a secular, non-religious private school in the area. She directly asked me whether there is another non-religious school that focuses on math and science. I can say that this school in this specific community is the only non-religious, private school that focuses on math and science education."

The principal of the GIS also said:

"We do not give any religious instruction here. However, I can say that we focus on universal values; including respect, integrity, dialogue, democracy. However, since our educational philosophy is based on those values, students naturally learn them. They learn informally from the teachers. However, it must be pointed out that the school administrators prepared a small prayer room in the size of approximately ten feet to twelve feet for their students. Any student from any religion was allowed to practice their prayers in this room."

The researcher's observations confirmed that students were using this simply-designed room for their Daily Prayers.

A Safe School Environment

Schools cannot ignore the security and safety concerns of all stakeholders, including parents, community members, school personnel, and students. Even a single violent incident can have dramatic consequences. Violence, at school or on the way to school, can affect the overall educational progress. No doubt the group most affected by this violence is the students. Violence increases student dropout rates, and affects the overall health of students' development (Fredland, 2008). The Center for the Prevention of School Violence in the North Carolina Department of Juvenile Justice and Delinquency Prevention (2011) defines school violence as "any behavior that violates a school's educational mission or climate of respect or jeopardizes the intent of the school to be free of aggression against persons or property, drugs, weapons, disruptions and disorder."

All interviewed GIS parents particularly emphasized their positive thoughts about the safe environment of the school. They cited the school's safe environment as one of the most important reasons why they chose the GIS for their children's education. All interviewed parents indicated that they hear of security issues at the other schools in the region. Two interviewed parents also indicated that they had sent their children to public schools in previous years. Although their children did not experience any safety-related incidents at those schools, these parents stated that they were worried about their children. School personnel also emphasized the school's safety as one of the most important characteristics that made the GIS different from other schools in the region. School administrators indicated that they were paying extra attention to safety concerns at the GIS in every stage of their students' education, from registration straight through to graduation. The principal of the GIS also emphasized that no serious safety-related incident had ever occurred at the school. The interviewed principal said:

"If a student has major problems, like ethical problems, or like drug usage, or those kinds of things, we draft and sign a contract with the student's parents and if the student continues these bad behaviors he will be expelled from the school. At the registration, we also orally explain how serious we are about inappropriate behaviors at the school."

The vice principal mirrored these thoughts:

"Security is a must. We are trying to get the safest environment here. And the reason is simple. If there is no security in a school there is no education. Bullying, including cyber bullying, is a real issue at the schools. And it is not easy to protect students from bullying. There are so many types of it. That's why we are organizing a lecture about cyber bullying, which is very common. And in the school we are very cautious. Any suspicious activity is investigated. You know sometimes bullying happens quietly. But the consequences can be dramatic."

According to all interviewed parents, the safe environment of the GIS was one of its unique characteristics, and when they were choosing the GIS for their children, they all considered this feature of the school. However, a safe environment has been reported by all interviewed parents as a secondary reason for their choice of the GIS, coming after the school's strong academic curriculum. One interviewed parent said:

"I am sending my child to this school because it also has a safe environment. No bullying and other things. If there are bad things happening in the school, you realize. You realize the change over your child's attitudes, over his face, of course, if you really care about your child. My child is happy at this school. I do double check. First, there are no awkward attitudes, and second, no bad grades. Furthermore, when you go to the school you see it with your own eyes. I also have to say that the teachers are very close to the students. If there is something wrong they do realize first and try to solve the problem."

Another interviewed parent added:

"I enrolled my son in one of the public schools before, and there were three or four security personnel you needed to pass to reach the secretary of the assistant principle. Security issues create barriers between people, including teachers and students. Then naturally, lack of educational success, even worse things may happen."

One of the strongest advantages of the school that contributes to its security was its relatively small number of students. The student-teacher ratio of the school was low and school personnel's control over safety issues was more effective. The Principal conceded that the size of the student body, 257 students, also contributes to the safe environment. The staff easily observes behavior and can intervene quickly in the event of a disruption. He added that:

"Our parents know how serious we are about safety in the school. And we are trying our best. Actually, things are happening naturally. I mean I think the safe environment is an outcome of our educational philosophy here. Dedicated teachers who really care about the students naturally bring safety. Teachers have close relationships with students and they know them well. And you know that students are spending hours in the school. And there are more than 170 students in this building without a security guard."

All interviewed parents expressed their positive thoughts about the school's safety by comparing the GIS with public schools in the region. They were aware of the safety problems at the public schools, and one interviewed parent cited examples of too much freedom, little control over students, drug usage, violence, and theft.

All interviewed parents also indicated that this safe environment is created by the school personnel's persistence. Furthermore, according to all interviewed parents, the faculty tries to protect the students as they would their sisters or brothers. In other words, a family-like environment promotes a safer environment at GIS. All interviewed parents said that they had a close relationship with the school's personnel and knew that the teachers were setting a good example with regard to good habits.

Other comments related to safety made by interviewed parents follow:

"Safety, I mean the rules in the school, they are designed to make sure that nothing dangerous, nothing criminal is happening in the vicinity of the school or inside the school. The people working there, you recognize them. They are dedicated, also they are dependable people, and their policy is to make sure the people they employ have no history of crime, drug addiction or other things that might hamper their teaching skills in the school. So they hire dependable, skilled individuals, and they make sure that the school environment is safe for the kids."

"I leave my student at school and I feel very comfortable. I know she will be looked after by the school personnel. If there is something wrong with my child, they do care about it as she was their sister or let's say their daughter. This builds a safe environment, naturally."

Why do parents send their children to schools? The primary purpose is in teaching them math, science, and literacy. The second purpose is children's socialization process. However, If you do not have a safe school both of those purposes cannot be accomplished. Furthermore, a child can learn reading, writing, math, and even history at home. Socialization is very important as through it they learn the values of respect, integrity, and responsibility, and learn to effectively interact with their peers. In an unsecure school you cannot teach those values, you cannot even teach math and literacy.

None of the interviewed parents talked about any security problems (i.e. drug usage, violence and fights) when the researcher asked the specific interview question of "If any, how have conflicts with your child's school personnel been effectively resolved? Any specific examples do you have?" The conflicts were more about the school buildings' physical features. For instance, concern was expressed about the small gym area at the GIS and the lack of extra facilities, such as a pool and a soccer field.

Observations also confirmed that the school had a safe atmosphere for all school personnel and for students. The researcher did not notice any suspicious activity during his visits to the school buildings. However, the researcher did notice that there were several security cameras in and outside the school, and that the principal's secretary was monitoring these cameras. There was also no security guard and no custodian working at the school buildings. The GIS's administrators indicated that teachers are assigned to monitor the students during lunch hours and breaks. Teachers are also assigned during specific times and for specific locations (i.e. cafeteria and front yard). At the school building housing grades 4 through 12, the main door was always locked, so that if someone wanted to enter the school, he used the intercom to notify the secretary, who then unlocked the door from her office. The secretary was also able to see the main door from two angles. The relatively small front yards at both school buildings were also surrounded by iron fences.

The principal of the GIS indicated that they invite professionals to give lectures about diverse topics at the school, including drug and alcohol abuse, violence, and bullying. In past years, for instance, the school administration had invited professionals from the Health Department to talk about drug and alcohol addiction. They have also invited officers from the local police department to talk about violence and theft. During this case study, the researcher participated in a lecture event where a professional from the police department visited the school to talk about cyber bullying. Attendance was mandatory for all middle and high school students. Some parents were also at the event, and listened to the lectures with their children. According to the principal, those speeches were very helpful in creating a safe and healthy environment for the students. The principal of the GIS also indicated that the speeches influenced student behavior.

The school also organized visits to the township's police department. The principal said the following:

"I believe that it is important [for the students] to see a professional person giving a lecture in the school. Those people know the real world and they know what is happening outside the school. They tell so many real stories. And those stories include students like our students. They tell what happens if bad behaviors continue. And telling a story with real examples is always more effective than what we and parents tell them."

Interviewed parents were also aware of the lecture activities on security issues. All interviewed parents prioritized presentations on security issues as one of the most important activities that the school administrators organized during the school year. One interviewed parent said he attended at least one of the lectures each semester. One interviewed parent also commented on these lectures:

"I hear about those lectures from my child. She likes to talk about those lectures. I think she likes to teach me what is really happening in the real world. What those professional people tell is about the real world, and sometimes includes very sad stories about the children who are involved in crime. I believe that students listen to them and take the advice seriously. Those lectures are very effective, and I hope they continue."

Another issue regarding the security at the GIS was the diverse backgrounds of the students. Although almost all students were born in the U.S., their ethnic backgrounds include Arabic, Spanish, Turkish, Pakistani, Hindu, and Greek. The researcher did not notice any problems among students based on ethnic backgrounds, nor was he informed about any such conflict. The interviewed vice principal of GIS indicated potential problems that might be caused by diversity in schools. The interviewed vice principal said:

"This area is a very cosmopolitan area and different ethnic groups are living here. Different languages are spoken. [It is] probably one of the most diverse regions of the U.S. Diversity is a value of richness. We carefully monitor students, and never let any illegal item in the school."

One interviewed parent reiterated the vice principal's comments:

"This area is very diverse. [GIS] is has a rich diversity. Arab, Spanish, Turkish, whites, blacks attend this school. Diversity is richness, but not always. There are potential conflicts, especially at schools. We are sure that there is no bullying at [GIS]. I know that, since there are close relationships between teachers and students at [GIS]."

Diversity at the GIS is not limited to the students' ethnicity but also the religious backgrounds of the students. Most students, as indicated by the school administrators, came from Muslim families. However, there were several Christian students studying at the GIS and, in limited numbers, there were Buddhist students at the GIS. The principal of the school said the following:

"We have mostly Muslim students, but there are Christian students and some from other religions. We do not choose any student [for enrollment based on] his religious background. There might be some concerns that religious diversity might cause some conflicts among the students. I honestly should say that there is nothing close to this [that has] happened in our school. As we talked previously, our educational philosophy is based on respect, respect to others. And we are very proud of our diversity at [GIS]."

One interviewed parent also mentioned the ethnic and religious diversity of the school with respect to security issues:

"We are a Muslim family. I know that at [GIS] there are students who come from Christian families. People might think that there are potential problems for such [a] school regarding the diversity. We do not see any problem. There are Christian and Muslim teachers. There is a harmony."

From the conversations with interviewed school personnel and interviewed parents, the researcher recognized that safety and security are based on the value of respect that is an essential part of Gülen's interfaith-intercultural dialogue perception.

Strong Value of School, Family and Community Relationships

According to Aslandogan and Cetin (2007), the relationship among school, community and family is one of the most important values of Gülen's educational philosophy. Gülen states (2000a) that family is vital to children's education. However, Gülen (2000a) also indicates that community should also be involved in the education since there are shared benefits and responsibilities. Moreover, the students who graduate from the schools become members of the community in the future. In other words, success of a school creates success in society. The data of this study reveals the last theme as the strong value in school, family, and community relationships. There were several indicators that the school places great emphasis on a strong relationship with parents and the community in order to better the education of its students. Interviewed school administrators and teachers made several references to activities designed to promote and to strengthen the bonds with the families and the community. The researcher participated in some of these activities that included parents and community members.

Observations and pertinent documents showed that various GIS activities took place at different locations, including the school's buildings, parents' houses, hotels, theaters and government buildings. In general, the activities at the school can be divided into two groups. The first group of activities included formal activities that included a large number of participants, for instance, lectures, dinners, and exhibitions. The second group of activities included less formal activities that are mostly scheduled later in the semester. Examples of this type of activity included home visits, community leader visits, and community department visits (e.g. police department and helping hand organizations). Additionally, school administrators explained that some activities were run by student clubs at the GIS.

Both interviewed school administrators indicated that the GIS places special emphasis on establishing partnerships with other stakeholders. According to them, it is necessary to reach out to not only the parents, but also to the whole community in order to better the education of students at the GIS. There were three major goals of extracurricular activities: to show how the school is operating with respect to their educational philosophy, to enhance the GIS students' social and academic development, and to involve other stakeholders (i.e. family and community members) in the education process. The principal

noted there were several strategies and plans to involve other stakeholders in the school's activities:

"We have a school policy for the activities that include parents
and community members. We plan most of them at the beginning of
the semester. I cannot count how many activities we do in a year but
[it] can go up to fifty. You know that different activities require different strategies before and during the activities. I mean family visits
are different from cultural day trips."

The principal of the GIS also emphasized that some activities were
organized and run by the students. The specific goal of one student club
was to strengthen the bond between the school and the community.

It is very important for a school to have connections with the
important people around, and so for that reason we established a club
that we call "Office Club". So, there is one teacher with the students
and he is guiding them. They visit important people in the community. For example, the mayor, fire chief, police chief, in their places of
work, and talk about our school philosophy, about our school success, and then invite them to our school. Students learn the meaning
of responsibility in practice.

The interviewed vice principal of the GIS also said that they invite
community leaders for lecture series and the school students benefit
from the relationships. The vice principal indicated that they were
striving for a mutual relationship with the other stakeholders:

"We also invite our community leaders as keynote speakers for
our leadership lecture series. They inspire our students for their future
career planning. I also should say that our school is contributing to the
community. Even before the graduation, students are becoming responsible citizens. They engage with the real life. Also our parents are
helping us with fundraising and some other activities in the parent-
teacher organization. So our parents and our community leaders are
actively involved in our school activities.

The lecture series included speakers with diverse backgrounds. During the spring of 2011, lectures were given by a journalist, an FBI agent,
the mayor of the city, a historian, a college professor, two agents from
the Health Department, and an agent from the Department of Home-

land Security. The topics of lectures in this series were naturally diverse too. The school also organized a panel discussion about the importance of language learning. Further, at the end of the 2011 spring semester, the former president of Tanzania gave a forty-five minute lecture about leadership at the school."

Researcher's observations confirmed that community members and parents were attending those events. However, parent-community involvement was not limited to the lecture series. The school also encouraged other stakeholders to participate in events at the school. Science fairs and helping hand activities also involved parents and community members. School administrators indicated that there were several clubs and competition teams at the school, and that their activities were also increasing the number of family and community participants.

Community and parent involvement in school events was not limited to their attendance as guests. Examples have been given about parents and community members' help and involvement before and during the school activities. The school principal emphasized that they want parents and community members' real involvement as organizers.

One specific example of community involvement was given by the interviewed computer science teacher who directs the Robotics Club. Club members participated in a statewide robotics competition. The interviewed computer science teacher said:

"I supervise the robotics club in the school. We don't have all the facilities in the school. We need to cut metal, we need to do some precise jobs with metal that we can't do in the school. So, for that reason I need to go out and find people [to help]. So we asked a lot of people from the robotics community. We ended up with volunteers working for us. For example, one computer engineer, an MIT graduate, worked with us until five in the morning. And there was a machine shop down there. And the person…was spending his weekends…He was spending his time with us and trying to get things done for the competition. We have a good relationship with the people. They give us their support because they see that we are working really hard."

Both interviewed school administrators highlighted that they were in touch with companies, government offices, churches and other schools in the region. Another example regarding the school-community relationship was given by an interviewed math teacher at the GIS:

"I can think of the dinners with the church that owned our school building. Last year we used to have those dinners, and the crowd was so welcoming and listened to us. I mean in this state, it's not like that. Unfortunately people are in distance. It was my second year in this state, and we used to have dinners every month. The first Thursday of every month we used to come together with church people. We used to talk about our religions. I remember we once had the ladies in the church and they took us inside the church. We were having the dinners in a specific room that was attached to the church and they were having a wedding ceremony. They started explaining to us the wedding ceremony; the rituals, and prayers. Then we started explaining how wedding ceremonies happen in Turkey. So it was like shared talk about our religion and culture. We found a lot in common about our religion and their religion."

Besides the lectures, in the spring semester of 2011, the school organized more than fifteen events in the school building, including a thanksgiving dinner, a poetry night, a science night, a family night, a talent show, and a science fair. Outside events also included trips, visits to community leaders, churches, temples, and mosques. Further, the school administrators also emphasized that students participated in community service projects at nursing houses, soup kitchens, veteran houses and hospitals. The principal of the GIS said the following:

"We also schedule community service programs for our students. This is very important. They go to nursing houses and hospitals. They attend food drive activities. They also work for helping hand organizations."

The vice principal added additional thoughts:

"We want our students to be responsible individuals in society, not only in the future but also during their school years. So we also specially schedule service learning activities, and they learn a lot during those activities. The reflections are insightful. Most of our teachers require students to prepare research papers or reflection papers about the activities. We want all of our middle and high school students to attend those service learning activities."

Both interviewed administrators said that several students attended such interfaith dialogue activities. During the spring semester of 2011, the students visited four churches, one synagogue and one mosque. The GIS principal explained that during the visits students were given brief lectures about various religious perspectives:

"Our students also visit churches, temples and mosques in the region. We want them to meet with the diversity in the society including religious diversity. We take interfaith dialogue seriously. A globalized world requires that. We believe that such dialogue brings peace, understanding and mutual respect."

Another important component of the parent-school bond was the family visits that are made by the school teachers. At the GIS, school administrators required all teachers to visit all the parents of their students. Moreover, as the vice principal stated, all initial family visits have been completed before the first semester of the educational year. By September of 2010, for example, all parents had been visited by the teachers in preparation for the 2010-2011 academic year. According to the interviewed administrators, family visits continued during each semester, and the average number of visits was about 2 per family. School administrators indicated that those early visits were demonstrative of how serious the school was about parental involvement. Furthermore, the teachers observed the home environments, and found more opportunities to offer suggestions to parents about improving the academic and disciplinary success of their children. The interviewed school administrators also indicated that the reflections of those visits were very positive and had a positive impact on the academic success of the students.

The principal said:

"We also advertise. I mean that we publicize our school. The best way to make the school well known in the area is this. Our parents are part of the society. The number is huge if you also add their relatives and friends. And they do the advertisement of our school. I mean every parent would like to talk about their kids. And the school is a very important place in their life. If they are happy with the school they talk positively. If they are not happy they talk negatively. Those family visits are the best opportunity to tell everything about the school. As a side benefit, we receive more applications."

The vice principal said the following:

"Some family visits include the student's peers from his class. They all go together for dinners, barbeque, or only for tea. This way we get more impact on students and of course on the families. They see us as a family."

All interviewed parents confirmed that they had been visited at least once before the start of the first semester. Four out of six parents said that they had been visited two times. All second visits had occurred during the first semester. All interviewed parents expressed their appreciation for those visits including one parent who shared their experience:

"They do have those family visits. I mean they came to our home before the semester started. This is a very valuable action that shows how serious they are about my child's education. The best part of those visits I think that they add some other students into the group. Once, my child's classmates came with their teacher. We had a dinner together."

Another interviewed parent said:

"They called me and said we would like to visit you whenever you are available. I was really surprised, and they came to my house and we talked about education. They talked about what they do at the school for the kids. They asked questions like how many hours my child was spending on the internet. They prepared a plan for him, like a time frame. You cannot find such care in any other school in the region."

Another interviewed parent said the following:

"It was Ramadan and my son's teacher came for an *iftar* dinner with some students. I do not remember how many came maybe around ten. As expected, we talked about education, how the students were doing at the school, their future plans, the activities at the school. But that happened in an informal format. This is unique. I believe that this is why this school is successful. I also think that this is good for the students. I mean that they do those visits together. They see the value of being a family I think. I think that this creates better friendships among the students."

All the interviewed parents asserted that these home visits were having a positive effect on their children's behavior and overall education. They also agreed that the best way to cultivate bonds between them and the school was the use of home visits. Two interviewed parents said that their day time jobs were not allowing them to remain involved in their children's education. They were only attending one or two parent-teacher meetings each semester. They saw these visits as a great opportunity for them to learn about the school's overall progress and about their children's education. One such interviewed shared their observations:

"I am a little bit busy with my job, and I obviously can not involve in all school activities. But those visits are helping me to learn how things are going at the school and how my child is doing at the school. This is a great school action to build good relationship with the parents. And I do not think this is happening in any other school in this area."

All the interviewed teachers indicated that the visits were very helpful in creating relationships with the parents. Interviewed teachers also indicated that family visits were an effective way to get parents more involved in their children's education. They believe that family visits cause parents to become more interested in the school and in school activities that include parents and other community members. Further, several benefits of these visits have been explained by all interviewed teachers. The first benefit, indicated by all interviewed teachers, was that the visits had a positive impact on students' educational and disciplinary success. All interviewed teachers stated that the level of attention paid by students to course subjects increased after these visits. In addition, they all indicated that students became more comfortable asking questions during and after class ours. One interviewed teacher said that "they [teachers] have a stronger relationship and connection with the parents and also with the students, and we can see the immediate effects on the students."

Another interviewed teacher said the following:

"Students see us as one of their family members, especially after those family visits. It is very easy to notice the difference before and after visits. Simply, they are involved [in] discussions more, they prepare better homework...They know that we, the teachers, do not hesitate to contact their parents about any concerns."

Another benefit of family visits indicated by all interviewed teachers was that they were able to learn more about a student's background and family environment. All interviewed teachers said that teachers are afforded greater opportunity to get to know families in their homes, since parents tend to speak in a more straightforward manner under their own roof. According to all interviewed teachers, parents were talking more freely about their educational concerns during these visits. Further, parents were asking more specific questions about their child's progress. At the same time, teachers were also able to ask specific questions about the students. One interviewed teacher responded that "Parents are able to ask specific questions about their educational concerns."

Another interviewed teacher said the following:

"We learn more about the families. We see the students' home environment. Even learning how many TVs and computers they have in the home is a clue. Of course we ask what students do at home after coming from the school. We learn what exactly we need to know. I mean parents speak freely."

Issues and Concerns

The hiring process at the GIS was not different than those at other private and public schools in the region. The vice principal indicated that they were using similar resources during the process of hiring teachers. The principal of the GIS noted that there was no orientation program about the values of Gülen's educational philosophy during the hiring process. All interviewed teachers confirmed that they did not attend any orientation program at GIS regarding Gülen's educational philosophy. All interviewed teachers and administrators had different stories about being an employee at this particular Gülen-inspired school. The principal of the school said that he started teaching in Mongolia thirteen years ago. He also worked at one of the Gülen-inspired schools in Poland. After working in Poland he ended up in the U.S. as a principal of the GIS. The principal indicated that he could have gone back to Turkey after Poland, but that he personally wanted to come to the U.S. When he was moving from one country to another, his personal connections helped him to decide what to do in order to teach and administer effectively at these schools. Meanwhile, one interviewed teacher said that after graduating from a U.S. college, he applied for a teaching position at a specific Gülen-inspired school. He, too, personally chose to become a teacher, rather than work for his family's business. Another interviewed teacher said her husband was a teacher in Turkey, and that they came to the U.S. after receiving their green card from the U.S green card lottery. Her husband started at another school in the region, and she had been helping his students as a tutor. A few years later, she completed her qualifications to become a teacher in the state and started working at the specific Gülen-inspired school. Yet another interviewed teacher said that he was working on his PhD in education and working at the school at the same time. He worked and taught at U.S. colleges before coming to the GIS. One of his friends recommended him to apply for a specific teaching position at GIS.

Interviews revealed that there was no single specific source that provided employees and workers for GIS. As the principal of GIS indicated that the most important values that they looked for in potential teachers were altruism and dedication to teaching. After these values they naturally looked for the quality of experience and teaching ability.

All interviewed school personnel also had different stories about learning about Gülen's educational philosophy and the Gülen Movement. Four interviewed teachers had themselves attended Gülen-inspired schools, while the other two did not. However, every interviewed teacher reported that they had read many books about Gülen in order to understand his philosophy and worldview. Further, all interviewed teachers said that they have listened to Gülen's speeches, which have been recorded since the late 1970s.

Four interviewed teachers indicated that they learned the English language after coming to the U.S. Some spent approximately two years learning English and improving their language skills before becoming a teacher at the GIS. Observations and interviews confirmed that the teachers were speaking fluent English and had no difficulty on expressing their thoughts.

All interviewed parents emphasized that the school building is not large enough for their students. Specifically, they complained about the small gym area, which is also used as a multipurpose space. Lack of sporting facilities was also highlighted by all interviewed parents. School administrators echoed these complaints, and noted that they were looking for a bigger and more functional school building in the region. The school administrators pointed out the rapid increase of the student body at the GIS as an explanation for the shortage of physical space. Further, they said that a real estate company had identified a larger school building for GIS, and that the school would probably be relocated within the next few years.

Since the GIS is an independent school, school administrators can be selective during the admission process. Although an entrance exam was administered, exam scores were used to assess the academic level of new students, and not to filter out students who score poorly. School administrators explained that they were trying to determine the academic level of a potential student in order to preserve homogeneity in the classrooms. Further, they indicated that students who scored well on the entrance exam were given different elective course objectives and a different schedule than students who received lower scores.

Both school administrators noted that they do not offer any religious instruction in their curriculum. They stated that a small room has been designated for prayers. The principal of GIS indicated that this room was nondenominational, and that any student who wanted to pray was able to use this room. Observations confirmed that some students were using this room for their prayers.

Summary

To answer the broad research question, this case study has proceeded by describing qualitative procedures for the data collection and analysis, then giving an overview of the Gülen-inspired School (GIS) in the United States. The study highlighted its mission and historical background, and then gave a summary of the research responses, which centered around four main themes.

Four emerged themes explain the characteristics of GIS with respect to its curriculum, history, success, hiring process, admission process and networking. The curriculum of GIS was not so different from curricula at other schools, but has been modified with respect to the students' needs. Further, all stakeholders agreed that the school had a science-oriented curriculum and that most of its numerous awards were from science Olympiads and fairs. Meanwhile, it must be emphasized that the school has developed rapidly, and that its fourteen-year history has been a successful one. The number of enrolled students and the academic success of these students were both highly noticeable, and showed that the school is progressively growing and succeeding.

The success of the school was very concrete. There were several indicators regarding the success of the school. The first important indicator was students' university placement, which was one-hundred percent for the last four years. In the 2010-2011 academic year, seventy-five percent of the GIS high school graduates were placed in the nation's top 50 colleges and universities. Concurrently, the school received several medals from diverse competitions at state and national levels. Further, during the last fourteen years, there was no serious disciplinary record or dropout at GIS. No doubt, the primary reason for the school's success was its dedicated teachers, who see their jobs as a noble occupation.

The hiring process was similar to those of other schools in the region. At GIS, there were teachers who studied at and graduated from other Gülen-inspired schools around the world. On the other hand, there were teachers who did not graduate or study at one of those schools. However, every interviewed teacher knew about the Gülen Movement on some level. School administrators indicated that they looked for quality and dedication in candidates during the process of hiring teachers for the school.

The admission process was also similar to those of the other private schools in the region. Since GIS is an independent school, they had the right to choose their potential students. The school administered a placement test to every potential student in order to ascertain the student's academic level. Accordingly, the GIS was creating homogeneity for its classrooms.

Networking at GIS was very unique to the school. GIS administrators indicated that they were trying to reach every parent for better educational success. Accordingly, all parents have been visited before the start of every fall semester. Teachers also accompanied their students to visit community leaders, non-profit organizations, companies and government offices. Further, several activities have been designed to involve all stakeholders in the GIS's networking.

Finally, as a new school, GIS is a developing institute that trying to prove itself in the region. The hardest work in this development, no doubt, has been done by its school personnel. In fourteen years, the school has shown progressive development with respect to its academic and disciplinary success. Further, school enrollment has increased more than tenfold. As the school administrators indicated, they were looking forward to moving the school to a larger building nearby. They also stated that they assume a larger and better school complex will contribute to the development of school in the future.

CHAPTER 5

Discussion and Conclusions

This study was designed to describe a Gülen-inspired school (GIS) in the United States and sought to explore how Gülen's educational philosophy is reflected in a Gülen-inspired school. This study identified the characteristics of a U.S. based GIS in terms of the school's curriculum, history, success, hiring process, admission process and networking. The researcher collected data through interviews, observations and reviewed pertinent documents of the school that described the fundamental nature of the experiences of administrators, teachers, and parents. Using a qualitative study approach, the researcher sought to gain deeper insight into the school from its founding to the present day.

Discussion of Findings

The interviewed participants shared their experiences by responding to interview questions that were designed for a specific Gülen-inspired school. After the data analysis process, four prominent themes emerged from this case study: science emphasis in the curriculum, safe environment of the school, school personnel's altruism and dedication to teaching, and strong value of school, family, and community relationships.

A Strong Emphasis on Quality Science Education

Gülen's educational philosophy emphasizes the synthesis of the mind and the heart, tradition and modernity, the spiritual and the intellectual (Aslandogan & Cetin, 2007). Gülen also understands the conflict between science and religion. But according to Gülen's educational philosophy, science and religion, in other words reason and faith, can be harmonized without a conflict. Gülen states (Unal & Williams, 2000):

"Einstein said that science teaches us the relations between phenomena and how phenomena exist together under their specific conditions. He added that science, which consists of the knowledge of what already is, does not teach us what should be; only religion teaches us how things should be and to which goals we should aspire." (p. 45)

Gülen's emphasis on science consequently reflects itself on the Gülen-inspired schools around the world. Gülen-inspired schools are famous for excellent computer technology and science laboratories. Further, those schools emphasis the importance of math and science education (Ebaugh, 2009).

Parallel to Gülen's emphasis on science the first theme that emerged from the data analysis was the school's emphasis on its science curriculum. This theme emerged as the most repeated theme during the interviews by all participants. However, the school personnel specifically emphasized that the school has a science-oriented curriculum. Accordingly, the school's success is concentrated around science-oriented areas. With respect to the emphasis toward science at school, the principal of the GIS stated the following:

"Although the real emphasis on curriculum goes to science education, we try to keep the balance between social science and science education. Let's say it this way: We are good with the social science education, but really good with science education."

Further, all interviewed parents were aware of the emphasis on science education at the GIS. However, interviewed parents did not state that they were sending their children to the GIS because of the school's science-oriented education. Rather, they all pointed out that the school is offering a high-quality education for their children.

The science emphasis in the curriculum was often described in association with the practical modifications that have been made to the curriculum by the interviewed school teachers. School administrators encouraged teachers to make necessary changes for better and effective education at the school. One of the most important reasons for the modifications, as stated by the school administrators, was students' capability to learn more while they were in high school. The school's administrators indicated that they were making a difference, since they offer high-level science courses for their students, the AP courses in particular have been given as an example of these. Students who completed those courses were able to receive related course exemptions from their colleges. It was also mentioned that social science courses received less modification. According to the interviewed social science teacher and the administrators, there were less opportunities to work on the social subjects. Understandably they were making fewer modifications to their curricula in those areas.

All interviewed parents and school administrators indicated that one of the most important reasons for such success is hidden in the so-called 'teacher factor'. They emphasized that the teachers were exemplary individuals, well educated, intelligent, and caring, who dedicated themselves to education in an extraordinary way. This assertion was supported during the study, as teachers were observed staying at the school well after classes had ended for tutoring sessions and for club activities. With the school administrator's guidance, teachers were organizing and leading several education-oriented activities in order to further educational success at the GIS.

School Personnel's Altruism and Dedication to Teaching

One of the most important features of Gülen's educational philosophy is the acceptance of teaching as a noble occupation. Further, Gülen emphasizes altruism and dedication in teaching. To do so, an educator should eliminate selfishness and should establish a spirit of community service. Gülen recognizes teachers as the key builders of the future, and that the spirit of these architects of the future was their devotion (Aslandogan & Cetin, 2007). Parallel to Gülen's educational philosophy, it was easily noticeable that the notions of devotion and altruism were exemplified by the GIS's personnel. None of the interviewed school personnel mentioned that they became a teacher because of the salary that they earn from the school. Instead, all interviewed teachers indicated that they chose to be a teacher because they see teaching as a noble occupation. One of the interviewed teachers summarized his perspective on education:

"As a teacher at [GIS], I really don't take it as being an employee. It is like coming here doing something for what you believe in. It's not like an employee, and there is no such relationship. I can say it's like a family here. You wouldn't call yourself as an employee when you do something in your family—for your family—so this is the first thing I would say."

Further, there were other indicators that suggested that the teachers were devoted to education. For instance, they were staying at the school after regular class hours for tutoring sessions and club activities. Some tutoring sessions and club activities even included weekend hours. The GIS teachers were either not paid or received limited pay for those extracurricular activities, and none of the interviewed teachers complained about this issue. The school administrators also looked for dedication and altruism when they were hiring teachers at the GIS. The principal indicated that during the hiring process they looked for teachers who were at once dedicated and successful. The school administrators also emphasized that one of the features that differentiated the GIS from other schools was such characteristics in their teachers. The principal of GIS believed that they would not have accomplished such success in such a relatively short time if they had not had such dedicated teachers at the school.

All interviewed parents also noted the dedication of teachers, who work extra hours to help their students to improve both academically and socially. During the interviews, the parents frequently mentioned that teachers take care of students as if they were their own children. This attitude is greatly appreciated by the interviewed parents. Further, all interviewed parents echoed the sentiments of school administrators, expressing their belief that teachers at the GIS make the real difference in the school's success and reputation.

Safe Environment of the School

During their educational years, students spend hours with their peers at school, especially on weekdays. It could be argued that a situation in which so many students spend so many hours in the school environment requires extra attention to safety, since even a small percentage of violence can have dramatic consequences on learning and development outcomes. Unsafe environments at schools can affect the overall educational process as well as students' social development.

Although Gülen's educational philosophy does not specifically highlight the safe environment for education, one of the most important characteristics of the GIS was revealed as the safe environment that is provided for both students and for the school's personnel. This characteristic of the GIS is mentioned several times, especially by all the interviewed parents. All the parents mentioned the safety concerns that they harbored, and all agreed that the GIS is a safe school for their children. The researcher believed that the security concerns of the interviewed parents came from the region where the school is located. Since the region was cosmopolitan, crowded, and experiencing pronounced immigration, its crime rates were above the state's average. Speciically, interviewed parents compared the school's safety with other schools in the region. Two interviewed parents had previously sent their children to other schools in the region and already knew of the poor conditions in those schools. Four interviewed parents stated that they hear from their neighbors or relatives about security issues at other schools. The two security concerns on which parents placed particular emphasis were drug related violence and sexual abuse.

With respect to the safe environment theme at the school, the principal stated the following:

"Our parents know how serious we are about safety in the school. And we are trying our best. Actually, things are happening naturally. I mean, I think the safe environment is an outcome of our educational philosophy here; Dedicated teachers who really care about the students naturally bring safety. Teachers have close relationships with students and they know them well. And you know that students are spending hours in the school. And there are more than 170 students in this building without a security guard."

Observations made by the researcher supported the suggestion that school administrators and teachers were exercising extra vigilance to ensure the school's security. The school was organizing lectures and visits regarding safety issues. Parents were also invited to such programs. It must also be emphasized that the school's small number of students allowed administrators and teachers more control and observation over the students.

Strong Value of School, Family and Community Relationships

Gülen emphasizes collective consultation and work in his teachings (Gülen 2005). Collective consultation and work in the educational field are evident in the strong cooperation among the stakeholders including parents, school and community members. Such collective consultation and work were observed at the GIS. All interviewed faculty believed that strong connections with the families and community members brought success and reputation to their school. To keep the connections strong and active, school personnel followed a distinctive schedule that was very effective and successful. With respect to the school's active networking with other stakeholders, the principal of the GIS stated the following:

"We have a school policy for the activities that include parents and community members. We plan most of them at the beginning of the semester. I cannot count how many activities we do in a year but [it] can go up to fifty."

Without doubt, the most important and transformative activity which reflects Gülen's educational philosophy was the family visits. Teachers visited the homes of all families before and during the semesters. These informal meetings have been mentioned by all interviewees. All interviewed parents expressed their appreciation with regards to those family visits. All interviewed parents indicated in particular that such visits were helping them to understand the overall educational practices that are provided by the GIS. On the other hand, interviewed GIS administrators indicated that such visits were providing effective parental involvement for future programs at school. According to the interviewed administrators, parents were becoming more involved in their children's education and the overall success of the school was increasing in kind. Besides those family visits, the school organizes several on-campus and off-campus events. Such events included trips, dinners, contests, and fundraising ventures. The primary goal of these events was to promote the students' social development. However, there were several side benefits of those activities. For instance, the GIS has invited all parents and several community leaders to science fairs organized by the school; in so doing, the school was informally publicizing itself and attracting future students. Further, those intensive extra activities were positively affecting the school's reputation. Activities such as lectures, dinners, and community leader visits were also making the school well known in the region. Parents became more involved in their children's education through those activities.

Conclusions

Two conclusions surfaced from this case study of a Gülen-inspired school in the United States. Firstly, it revealed themes of the study rooted in Gülen's four dimensional education philosophy. In other words, the Gülen's educational philosophy reflected itself in the revealed themes as related to the GIS's curriculum and in its internal culture. Academic success with a strong focus on science education was at the core of the curriculum. Parallel to the scholars (Mehmeti, 2009; Santos 2006; Woodhall, 2005) who investigated Gülen-inspired schools around the world, this study agrees that the GIS can be defined as a science-oriented school. Further, cooperation among all stake holders was also a significant indicator that the school was following Gülen's educational philosophy. On the other hand, teachers' noble perspective on their occupation was also an indicator that the school is founded on Gülen's educational philosophy.

Secondly, the case study illustrates well what can happen when a school promotes and takes advantage of "social capital" as defined by Cohen and Prusak (2001, p. 4). The evidence of shared values and trust made cooperative actions possible for the benefit of the students. Such social capital contributed to the academic success and the strong reputation of the school. Furthermore, the observed harmony and the cooperation among the GIS's school personnel strengthened the existing social capital. GIS administrators utilized and promoted social capital which resulted in a strong partnership among teachers, parents, and community members.

Implications of the Study

The research generated information about many aspects of a Gülen-inspired school in the U.S. (i.e. the school's curriculum, history, success, hiring process, admission process and networking). The results of this research can be utilized to inform practice and improve schools. Multiple audiences, including educators and policy makers, can also benefit from the findings of this study.

First and foremost, this research argues for the importance of the school, parent and community relationship, which was very dynamic at the GIS. The school's strategies to make parents especially involved in their children's education were quite unique to the school. Here the research indicates a correlation between the strong linkages with stakeholders (i.e. the school, parents, and community members) and the school's success, as reflected in graduates' acceptance to selective universities and the school's performance in national and international competitions. Different activities that included parents and community members also positively affected all stakeholders' views of the school. Activities also affected the school's reputation positively in the region. Out of all the different types of activities, the home visits in particular were very helpful in motivating parents and students. Further, this specific activity was also very motivating for the teachers. Accordingly, such a simple activity can be transferred to improve overall academic and disciplinary success in any other school in the U.S.

Additionally, the school teachers' modifications to course subjects for better educational success were unique and can be applicable to other schools in the U.S. The benefits of such modifications were indicated by all teachers at the GIS. It can be said that such a modification strategy can be applicable at some level at other schools with respect to the students' needs, as was done by the GIS's teachers.

Limitation of the Study

It is the very nature of qualitative studies to utilize small sample sizes during inquiry. Accordingly, the findings cannot be generalized. The most obvious limitation was the limited number of interviewed teachers and parents. The researcher interviewed six parents and six teachers. It is the researcher's belief that the interviews were persuasive. However, the reflections of those limited number of interviewees regarding the school may not be sufficient to explain the research question of this study.

The second limitation was the researcher's partial participation in the school's events. Although the researcher participated in several of the school's activities that also involved parents and community members, he could not attend all scheduled activities. Further, since this research has been conducted in the spring semester of 2011, the researcher did not attend the 2010's fall semester activities. As indicated by the GIS's administrators, the fall semesters' activities were more intensive and frequent.

Additionally, due to the specific characteristics of the region where the GIS's students come from, overall findings cannot be generalized for other Gülen-inspired schools around the world. The region where the school was located was culturally diverse. Several ethnic groups were sending their children to the GIS. This exceptional characteristic of the school limits the ability to generalize findings.

Finally, since the school personnel who worked at the GIS in the past have not been interviewed, a sufficient reflection on the historical development of the school cannot be claimed.

Recommendations for Future Research

The unique characteristics of the region where the GIS is located lead the researcher to make his first recommendation for the future research. Since this particular Gülen-inspired school is located in an urban area where different ethnic and religious groups live and continuously migrate to, researching other Gülen-inspired schools in the U.S. can give different conclusions and results with respect to their curriculum, history, success, hiring process, admission process and networking. In other words, research is needed to determine how other Gülen-inspired schools are operated in different cultural contexts and in different geographical locations in the U.S. Different studies on different Gülen-inspired schools can be compared for better understanding about the schools' overall success and their internal cultures. Also, more data, both quantitative and qualitative, is needed to compare the Gülen-inspired schools with other private schools and with government schools throughout the U.S. Further, the future studies about the Gülen-inspired schools may include the voice of their students with respect to their experience in those schools.

This study focused mostly on the secondary school, where the emphasis is primarily on science and mathematics education. Additional studies focusing on the Gülen's educational philosophy could look into whether his ideas could be beneficial in the social sciences areas and in elementary education.

Additional research can be conducted about the specific school's graduates, who will continue their education in diverse higher education institutions around the world. Since the school has only graduated high school seniors for the past four years, their success at college with respect to the education that they received from the GIS can be researched.

APPENDICES

APPENDIX A

Institutional Review Board Approval

MARYWOOD UNIVERSITY
INSTITUTIONAL REVIEW BOARD
O'Neill Center for Healthy Families, 2300 Adams Avenue, Scranton, PA 18509

DATE:	February 8, 2011
TO:	Erkan Acar
FROM:	Marywood University Institutional Review Board
STUDY TITLE:	[204301-4] *Case Study of a Gülen Inspired School in the United States*
MUIRB #:	2010-058
SUBMISSION TYPE:	Amendment/Modification
ACTION:	APPROVED
APPROVAL DATE:	February 8, 2011
EXPIRATION DATE:	February 8, 2012
REVIEW TYPE:	Expedited Review
EXPEDITED REVIEW TYPE:	45 CFR 46.110 (b)(1)(5, 6 and 7)

Thank you for your submission of Amendment/Modification materials for this research study. Marywood University's Institutional Review Board has **APPROVED** your submission. This approval is based on an appropriate risk/benefit ratio and a study design wherein the risks have been minimized. All research must be conducted in accordance with this approved submission.

This submission has received Expedited Review based on the applicable federal regulations.

Please remember that <u>informed consent</u> is a process beginning with a description of the study and assurance of participant understanding, followed by a signed consent and/or assent form. Informed consent must continue throughout the study via a dialogue between the researcher and research participant. Federal regulations require each participant to receive a copy of the signed consent document.

Only the stamped, approved consent forms and letter may be used in this research.

Please be aware that all research records must be retained by the researcher for a minimum of three years.

Please also note that:

- Any revision to previously approved materials must be submitted to, and approved by, the IRB prior to initiation.
- All SERIOUS and UNEXPECTED adverse events must be reported to this office. All FDA and sponsor reporting requirements should also be followed.
- All NON-COMPLIANCE issues or COMPLAINTS regarding this study must be reported to this office.
- Researchers must submit a status report 6 months from the date of approval. Your first status report is due on or before **August 8, 2011**. A final status report is due prior to **February 8, 2012**, unless you are applying for renewal/continuing review.
- Federal regulations require research to be reviewed no less than annually; therefore, research activities may not continue beyond the expiration date until submitted to, reviewed and approved by the IRB. Renewal applications should be submitted at least 60 days prior to your study's expiration date. Failure to obtain approval for the renewal of your study prior to the expiration date will require discontinuance of all research activities, including recruitment of participants, enrollment of new participants, data collection and data analysis. To renew, please submit a Continuing Review application along with all required materials via IRBNet.

The appropriate forms for any of the reports mentioned above may be found at http://www.marywood.edu/irb/ or in the Forms and Reference Library on IRBNet.

If you have any questions, please contact the IRB Office at 570-961-4782 or irb@maryu.marywood.edu.

Please include your study title and MUIRB number in all correspondence with this office.

Thank you and good luck with your research!

APPENDIX B

Consent Form for School Administrators

How is the philosophy of a "Gülen-inspired school" reflected in a United States based GIS, as it relates to curriculum, history, success, hiring process, admission process and networking?

You are invited to participate in a research study to examine meaning of "Gülen-inspired school" at GIS. You were selected as a possible participant due to your relationship with the school as a school administrator. I ask that you read this for and ask any questions you may have before agreeing to be in the study. This study is being conducted as a dissertation by Erkan Acar, Ph.D. candidate completing his dissertation, at Marywood University.

Background Information

The purpose of this case study is to describe a Gülen-inspired school (GIS) in the United States in light of it guiding principles of altruism, accepting and appreciating the teaching as a noble action/vocation, synthesis between science and values, and the cooperation among the stakeholders. The study will identify the characteristics of a U.S. based GIS in terms of the school's curriculum, history, success, hiring process, admission process and networking.

Procedures

If you agree to participate in this study, you will receive another letter to specify time and place where we will have an interview. You will be asked 12 (twelve) open ended questions regarding the research

Risks and Benefits

This study has risks no greater than those experienced in daily life and activities. The benefits of participation are assisting this researcher in examining meaning of Gülen-inspired school in the U.S. Accordingly the study will help to understand a new educational approach to educational system of the U.S. You would be contributing to the advancement of knowledge in this area.

Confidentiality

The records of this study will be kept private. In any sort of report I might publish, I will not include any information that will make it possible to identify you. Research records will be kept in a locked file for 3 years; only the researchers will have access to the records. After 3 years period, records will either be deleted or shredded. Records will only be used for current study. The records will be transcribed by the researcher. The information that comes from the interviews will not be shared with the GIS.

Voluntary Nature of the Study

Your decision whether or not to participate will not affect any future relations with the researcher, Marywood University and GIS. If you decide to participate you are free to withdraw at any time without affecting those relationships. If you would like to withdraw from the study, your interview will not be used and all records will be deleted or shredded. You can let me know when you decide withdrawing either sending an e mail or by calling.

Contacts and Questions

The researcher conducting this study is Erkan Acar. You may ask any questions you may have now. If you have questions later, you may contact me at that time: phone (570) 801-3707; email: eacar@m.mary-wood.edu. You may also contact my advisor Mary Salvaterra Ph.D. for your questions, either from (570)-348-2338 or from salvaterra@maryu.marywood.edu. You will be given a copy of this form to keep for your records.

If you have any questions now or later, related to the rights of research subjects. You may also contact to Dr. Maria Montoro Edwards, Assistant Vice President for Research, Marywood University, at (570) 348 6211, extension 4775 or montoro@maryu.marywood .edu

Statements of Contents

I have read the previous information. I have asked questions and have received answers.

I consent to participate in the study.

Participant's Signature _____ _____ Date _____

Investigator's Signature_____Date_____

School Administrators' Interview Questions

Demographics

1) Title and certification. Number of years the person has worked in education.
2) Number of years the person has been employed in current position.

Interview Questions

1) How does the curriculum of GIS differ that offered in public schools? Please give specific examples.
2) Where did you learn about the philosophy of a Gülen-inspired school?
3) Tell me about your experiences as an employee in this Gülen-inspired school.
4) Tell me about your experiences at the time of your hire. Were you provided with an orientation on the values of Gülen-inspired school?
5) This school has a strong academic program. Share with me why you think it has been successful.
6) Successful schools build strong linkages with major stakeholders. Can you identify these stakeholders and explain how you build those strong linkages?
7) Talk about the activities that include parents and community members.

8) Can you describe the school's educational curriculum? Do you think it is effective?

9) Can you describe the school's role in the community?

10) Can you talk about the school's historical development?

11) How does the hiring process work for GIS? What are your criteria?

12) How do you admit your students? What are your criteria?

APPENDIX D

Consent Form for School Teachers

How is the philosophy of a "Gülen-inspired school" reflected in a United States based GIS, as it relates to curriculum, history, success, hiring process, admission process and networking?

You are invited to participate in a research study to examine meaning of "Gülen inspired school" at GIS. You were selected as a possible participant due to your relationship with the school as a teacher. I ask that you read this for and ask any questions you may have before agreeing to be in the study. This study is being conducted as a dissertation by Erkan Acar, Ph.D. candidate completing his dissertation, at Marywood University.

Background Information

The purpose of this case study is to describe a Gülen-inspired school (GIS) in the United States in light of it guiding principles of altruism, accepting and appreciating the teaching as a noble action/vocation, synthesis between science and values, and the cooperation among the stakeholders. The study will identify the characteristics of a U.S. based GIS in terms of the school's curriculum, history, success, hiring process, admission process and networking.

Procedures

If you agree to participate in this study, you will receive another letter to specify time and place where we will have an interview. You will be asked 7 (seven) open ended questions regarding the research topic. Interviews will take approximately 1 (one) hour. Our conversation will be recorded to a tape recorder.

Risks and Benefits

This study has risks no greater than those experienced in daily life and activities. The benefits of participation are assisting this researcher in examining meaning of Gülen-inspired school in the U.S. Accordingly the study will help to understand a new educational approach to educational system of the U.S. You would be contributing to the advancement of knowledge in this area.

Confidentiality

The records of this study will be kept private. In any sort of report I might publish, I will not include any information that will make it possible to identify you. Research records will be kept in a locked file for 3 years; only the researchers will have access to the records. After 3 years period, records will either be deleted or shredded. Records will only be used for current study. The records will be transcribed by the researcher. The information that comes from the interviews will not be shared with the GIS.

Voluntary Nature of the Study

Your decision whether or not to participate will not affect any future relations with the researcher, Marywood University and GIS. If you decide to participate you are free to withdraw at any time without affecting those relationships. If you would like to withdraw from the study, your interview will not be used and all records will be deleted or shredded. You can let me know when you decide withdrawing either sending an e mail or by calling.

Contacts and Questions

The researcher conducting this study is Erkan Acar. You may ask any questions you may have now. If you have questions later, you may contact me at that time: phone (570) 801-3707; email: eacar@m. marywood.edu. You may also contact my advisor Mary Salvaterra Ph.D. for your questions, either from (570)-348-2338 or from salvaterra@ maryu.marywood.edu. You will be given a copy of this form to keep for your records.

If you have any questions now or later, related to the rights of research subjects. You may also contact to Dr. Maria Montoro Edwards, Assistant Vice President for Research, Marywood University, at (570) 348 6211, extension 4775 or montoro@maryu.marywood .edu

Statements of Contents

I have read the previous information. I have asked questions and have received answers.

I consent to participate in the study.

Participant's Signature _____ _____ Date _____

Investigator's Signature_____Date_____

Appendix E

Teachers' Interview Questions

Demographics

1) Gender, age.
2) Number of years the person has been employed in current position.

Interview Questions

1) How does the curriculum of GIS especially in your major differ that offered in other public schools? Please give specific examples from your teaching area.
2) Where did you learn about the philosophy of Gülen-inspired school?
3) Tell me about your experiences as an employee in this Gülen-inspired school.
4) Tell me about your experiences at the time of your hire. Were you provided with an orientation on the values of Gülen-inspired school?
5) Can you talk about your relationship with your students' parents?
6) Can you talk about your personal experiences during the school activities with other stakeholders?

Consent Form for School Parents

H ow is the philosophy of a "Gülen-inspired school" reflected in a United States based GIS, as it relates to curriculum, history, success, hiring process, admission process and networking?

You are invited to participate in a research study to examine meaning of "Gülen-inspired school" at GIS. You were selected as a possible participant due to your relationship with the school as a parent. I ask that you read this for and ask any questions you may have before agreeing to be in the study. This study is being conducted as a dissertation by Erkan Acar, Ph.D. candidate completing his dissertation, at Marywood University.

Background Information

The purpose of this case study is to describe a Gülen-inspired school (GIS) in the United States in light of it guiding principles of altruism, accepting and appreciating the teaching as a noble action/vocation, synthesis between science and values, and the cooperation among the stakeholders. The study will identify the characteristics of a U.S. based GIS in terms of the school's curriculum, history, success, hiring process, admission process and networking.

Procedures

If you agree to participate in this study, you will receive another letter to specify time and place where we will have an interview. You will be asked 6 (six) open ended questions regarding the research topic.

Interviews will take approximately 1 (one) hour. Our conversation will be recorded to a tape recorder.

Risks and Benefits

This study has risks no greater than those experienced in daily life and activities. The benefits of participation are assisting this researcher in examining meaning of Gülen-inspired school in the U.S. Accordingly the study will help to understand a new educational approach to educational system of the U.S. You would be contributing to the advancement of knowledge in this area.

Confidentiality

The records of this study will be kept private. In any sort of report I might publish, I will not include any information that will make it possible to identify you. Research records will be kept in a locked file for 3 years; only the researchers will have access to the records. After 3 years period, records will either be deleted or shredded. Records will only be used for current study. The records will be transcribed by the researcher. The information that comes from the interviews will not be shared with the GIS.

Voluntary Nature of the Study

Your decision whether or not to participate will not affect any future relations with the researcher, Marywood University and GIS. If you decide to participate you are free to withdraw at any time without affecting those relationships. If you would like to withdraw from the study, your interview will not be used and all records will be deleted or shredded. You can let me know when you decide withdrawing either sending an e mail or by calling.

Contacts and Questions

The researcher conducting this study is Erkan Acar. You may ask any questions you may have now. If you have questions later, you may contact me at that time: phone (570) 801-3707; email: eacar@m.marywood.edu. You may also contact my advisor Mary Salvaterra Ph.D. for your questions, either from (570)-348-2338 or from salvaterra@maryu.marywood.edu. You will be given a copy of this form to keep for your records.

If you have any questions now or later, related to the rights of research subjects. You may also contact to Dr. Maria Montoro Edwards, Assistant Vice President for Research, Marywood University, at (570) 348 6211, extension 4775 or montoro@maryu.marywood.edu

Statements of Contents

I have read the previous information. I have asked questions and have received answers.

I consent to participate in the study.

Participant's Signature _____ _____ Date _____

Investigator's Signature_____Date_____

Appendix G

Parents' Interview Questions

Demographics
1) Gender, age.
2) Number of children who are attending to GIS, their grades and years of attendance.

Interview Questions
1) What do you think about your child's school? What attracts you to GIS?
2) What do you think about GIS's activities? Meetings, lectures, trips, etc.? Do you think that they are beneficial? Can you talk about any specific experience?
3) What have educators done to establish an effective team relationship with you?
4) What could be better with your child's school?
5) Are you familiar with the overall educational philosophy of your child's school?
6) If any, how have conflicts with your child's school's personnel been effectively resolved?

Appendix H

Gülen's Thoughts on Education

The Youth[1]

> Yours alone is this reform, this revolution.
> Does not everything belong to you, Oh youth?[2]

T he most important issues of our time concern the young generation. How do we give them what they are due and ask of
them what we need? It is essential that we take seriously both
the promises and the challenges of the coming generation.

The youth give shape to every change; they bring forth new eras.
The Roman revolution was theirs, and Hellenism was theirs. The
earth awaits the honor of their footsteps again, and the heavens listen
for their voices. The seven wonders of the world are pillars to youth's
magnificence. Their arching brows are crescent moons, and their
smiles are as bright and mysterious as stars. Do not think I exagger-
ate: Even a thousand eulogies could not describe the glory of these
young generations. Baqi says:

> The breezes of spring blew like the breath of Jesus,
> And the flowers opened their eyes from the sleep of nonexistence.[3]

---

[1] Gülen, M. Fethullah, "Gençlik," *Zuhur*, August 1977, Issue 3; Kurt, Erkan M., *A Fethullah Gülen Reader: So That Others May Live*, New Jersey: Blue Dome Press, 2013, pp. 109–112.

[2] Tevfik Fikret (d. 1915), Turkish-Ottoman poet.

[3] Baqi (d. 1600), Turkish-Ottoman poet.

If that magnificent poet of the Ottoman Empire had turned his gaze toward the youth—those who bring new life to us—he would similarly praise them.

Yet the ignorant consider the youth to be useless vagrants, and the advocates of anarchy enlist them as elements of destruction. But for us, the young generation represents incomprehensible potential. It is their nature to be lively and restless. If neglected, they will become a deadly poison. But when the young are rightly educated, their nobility is unsurpassed. Like heroes, they can overcome perils by the thousands. But they can also be made captives at the hands of lust. Everyone tries to lure the youth; everyone wants to obtain them. If you win their confidence, they will offer you relief and comfort. But if you don't hold them fast, they are easily carried off. If you offer them only vague ideals, any daydreamer can lead them astray. If you fix their minds on concrete things, they will become fetishistic. If you can free them from animal desires, they will acquire a second nature, but if you let them loose in the field of pleasures, they will crumble like a burned coal into nothing.

If you attend to them, the youth will rise to the summits, reciting:

> When you imbibe that wine of divine love,
> The light of the universe shines into your heart and gives you
> eternal life.[4]

But if you abandon them, they will fall into ruin, chanting:

> Drink the wine and love the beautiful, if you are wise.
> Do not care whether the world exists or not.[5]

The youth are pure potential. We must not neglect them, for they have not yet realized their nature. How can we neglect them? In our recent history, custody of the young was given to chauvinistic thinking.[6] Later, in a period of a total alienation, they were an unprec-

---

[4] Gedai (d. 1889), Turkish-Ottoman folk poet.
[5] Ziya Pasha (d. 1880).
[6] The author refers to the strict nationalism, enforced by the government in the early decades of the Turkish Republic.

edented disaster: spoiled and unchaste. And today, the young generation groans like a painful ulcer in the stomach or a cataract in the eye.
Their humanity is a fraud, their mercy is feigned, they spend themselves in deception, and their courage is an illusion. They are now dis-
figured, among the lowest of the low. However, the hand of a true
educator can still shape them; they can still achieve the high stature
that the universe has reserved for them. It is not too late for today's
youth to receive the divine favor.

They long for a teacher, who will lead them from the rank of nov-
ice to the heights of mastery. Then, they will understand what harm
the ignorant have done to them, and they will keep their distance
from such empty lives. They expect protection and discernment from
those who have gone before them, and we expect them to bring unity
to their hearts and minds and embrace their virtuous history. They wait
for a skilled doctor, who can cure the sickness that has gripped their
souls and provide a remedy for the delusions that have grown old in
their minds. They cry out, "Fire! Come to my help!" And we say, "Allow
us to put out this fire with our sweat."

Oh, the community of mercy![7] If you cannot wait for the Day of
Resurrection, then stand up! As Heracles rescued Prometheus, run to
the help of our youth, who suffer now under the illusions of their own
desires.

Elevating Humanity[8]

> Your essence is even loftier than angels.
> Realms are hidden in you, worlds compacted.[9]

Humanity is essentially the subject of every philosophical and scientific theory. No philosophy can be articulated, or any science developed,

---

[7]   Originally: *ümmet-i merhume*, a classical Turkish phrase to refer to the entire Muslim
    community. The phrase literally means: "the community upon which God has
    mercy."

[8]   Gülen, M. Fethullah, "İnsanı Yükseltme," *Sızıntı*, July 1979, Issue 6; Kurt, Erkan
    M., *A Fethullah Gülen Reader: So That Others May Live*, New Jersey: Blue Dome
    Press, 2013, pp. 113–116.

[9]   Mehmed Akif (d. 1936).

without first taking human beings into consideration. All study is an attempt to understand humanity in both its physical and metaphysical dimensions, for all other things have significance and value only in relation to humanity. All branches of the sciences gather around us to discuss our various aspects. Books hasten to us, fill themselves with us, and thus become radiant.

Human beings are so perfectly tuned, our biological functions so perfectly adjusted, that we manifest the ideal structure. We cannot help but admire the anatomy of our every organ, not to mention the eternally unfolding depths of our spiritual nature. An intricate brain and an ineffable spirit held together in perfect harmony! Every aspect of the human being is like a magnificent work of art, worthy of wonder. But here we will not deal with humanity's marvelous appearance or the inward dimensions beyond it, but on our unique potential and ability.

The human being in all his aspects is a difficult creature to understand. His peculiarities begin when he first enters the world. Other creatures possess perfect instincts and knowledge of the laws of life; they come into the world as if they had already been trained in another one. But the human being, the most magnificent and esteemed of all creatures, emerges without any knowledge and with none of the skills necessary for life. Beyond the mechanical order of his body, everything in him develops according to his reason, will, freedom, and introspection. In this way, his inner and outer existences are integrated, and he becomes a self. This capacity for synthesis is the greatness of humanity, but it can only be developed through education. If we were to simply leave humanity to its instincts, unable to realize the potential of its identity, this would be like leaving a seed without soil.

The lion is equipped with its paw and the bull with its horns, but humanity must prepare all means of survival for itself. We must use our intellect, will, and reason to invent what is beneficial and prevent what is harmful. In this way, we build a civilization in which we can find peace as individuals. Then future generations will inherit the works and virtues cultivated by the hearts and minds of all humanity. This is natural, for the human being is not concerned with the present alone. The past and the future are also present in his mind and essential to his existence. This is why the many contributors to the development of science and philosophy did not quit working, even when they knew they would not enjoy the fruits of their labor. They worked in the name of knowledge and culture for all humanity and left an astounding heritage behind them. Without such selflessness, there can be no civilization on earth.

But the efforts of past generations have given us more than just material development; they have also left us with a heritage of virtue. It is according to the wisdom of those who have gone before us that we develop our capabilities, plan our behaviors, and channel our efforts to good purpose. Throughout history, generations have always set themselves the task of educating subsequent generations, for education is the greatest gift they have to offer. Education fixes humanity's attention on lofty purposes and keeps us from the distraction of our animal inclinations. By providing a frame and context for our activities, education keeps us from wild degeneration. Through education, our capabilities are allowed to flourish, and we unearth the potential hidden in our soul.

In the heart of humanity, there are only seeds of goodness; therefore, even feelings like lust and anger can lead indirectly to beautiful outcomes. Through education, this becomes possible. In other words, only after our capacity for reason, will, and introspection are brought to fruition by education can we become truly human. Then we transcend our animal existence, achieve autonomy in nature, and bind ourselves to the Being of absolute independence.

Human reason, as defined by philosophy, is our ability to draw conclusions from given premises. This intellectual activity distinguishes us from the rest of creation. Reason is a special endowment to humanity, but we do not receive it in its mature form. It is ours only as a potential that we must develop. When reason is united with conscience, it gains a new identity as the link between our inner and outer existences. Then, our conscience guides our behavior. In this sense, the ultimate purpose and highest ideal of human reason is the attainment of the knowledge of God. With this knowledge, reason reaches maturity and perfection, and we come to know our moral responsibilities.

Freedom is a consequence of the autonomy we enjoy as humans. We have free control over our actions, but we are also uniquely accountable for them. One should reject the materialist understanding in which humanity's actions are fully determined like the movements of a machine, for it is impossible to discuss morality without first positing freedom. As moral creatures, we possess a dimension that is not determined by the laws of nature: Our conscience clearly signifies the existence of a transcendent realm, to which we are bound by our responsibility to differentiate right from wrong.

When we reflect upon the external world in our conscience, we catch a glimpse of what is beyond this realm of contingency. In contemplation, we are elevated beyond our spatial limitations. The degree of such "ascension" depends on the quality of our intellectual activity, the determination of our will, and the depth of our introspection. Every individual is capable of contemplation, and each of us can share in it according to our abilities. Ascension brings us to the ultimate attainment of the inner life: contemplation of the Creator's unique beauty.

For centuries, our people have neglected this lofty journey. But it is our duty, particularly as educators, to help the younger generations attain the knowledge of their human essence. We must nurture their reason and vitalize their will. We must help them purify their feelings and connect with what is beyond nature. If we do not raise the young to the dignity of their human potential, history will hold us responsible for their total alienation.

Our Philosophy of Education (I)[10]

The beginning of a new school year is a prudent time for us to re-examine our system of education. For a school is a vital laboratory of the future, its courses are the potions of life, and its teachers are the heroic masters of healing.

---

[10] Gülen, M. Fethullah, "Bizim Maarifimiz - I," *Sızıntı*, October 1979, Issue 9; Kurt, Erkan M., *A Fethullah Gülen Reader: So That Others May Live*, New Jersey: Blue Dome Press, 2013, pp. 117–120.

School is where we are taught everything about life and what lies beyond it. Of course, life itself is a place of learning, but it is only through school that we are introduced to this fullness of life. Education focuses the light of wisdom on life's events so that students can comprehend their environment. It illuminates the meaning of phenomena and brings integrity to our thoughts. Education gives our contemplation consistency and unifies creation's multiplicity. In this sense, a school is no different than a sanctuary, with the teachers its revered saints.

A good school is like a pavilion full of angels: It develops individual virtues and guides its students toward the dignity of their spirit. At a good school, children learn the mysteries of the self and realize their potential. But if pupils are imbued with vulgarity and alienated from each other, a school is nothing but a ruin. For some centuries now, such twisted institutions have been a cause for our embarrassment.

The true teacher sows and cultivates the seeds of virtue. He is attentive to that which is good and wholesome. He sets goals for the students and offers them direction in the face of life's vicissitudes. It is in school that life's abundant flow acquires a distinct identity. In other words, like a confluence of rivers, a school consolidates the plurality of life into a whole. It is in school that we train our minds to bring unity to the dispersion of life's events.

It would be a mistake to assume that school is only relevant during certain periods of life. On the contrary, school introduces students to a lifetime of study. In this respect, our education influences every part of our lives, even if we never spent much time in a classroom. When pupils learn the lessons concerning truth, they will spend their entire lives reviewing them. What is of importance is that we utilize such lessons as guides on our way to virtue.

At school, knowledge is internalized in the form of wisdom. This allows us to transcend the material dimension and touch the boundaries of infinity. Knowledge that is not internalized is an embarrassing burden loaded on our shoulders. It is like a mischievous devil that causes confusion. Indeed, rote learning that does not illuminate the mind or elevate the soul will only erode our conscience and weary our heart.

The best form of knowledge that a school can provide is one that imbues the phenomena of the external world with the wisdom of the inner world. A good teacher can transform what appear to be external phenomena into integral parts of our inner life. Undoubtedly, life itself is the greatest guide and the truest master, continually repeating its lessons. However, we need practice before we can enroll in these illustrious lessons, and this practice is what our teachers offer. They mediate between our life and our conscience, teaching us to interpret the subtle language of phenomena.

Books, newspapers, radio and TV can teach us some things, but they can never teach us the reality of life or its presence within us. In this respect, a good teacher is irreplaceable. Every day, he or she manages to bring new passion into our hearts and leave indelible impressions on our minds. There are many things that students can be taught easily with the aid of technology, but the crucial lessons address the purpose of knowledge and require the presence of qualified teachers, who bring their lessons forth from the prisms of their hearts. This is the secret of the many great teachers in human history.

A good lesson is one that is learned in the presence of such a teacher. The students not only enrich their knowledge; they are also brought to the threshold of infinite unknown realities, to the point of enlightenment. Through our lessons, we begin to grasp the natural world as a lace curtain through which we contemplate eternal truths, or as a veil laid over the realms of mystery. In such a school, no one can ever get enough of learning. For teachers enjoy leading their pupils to the stars and bringing them to rest in their consciences. This is a kind of education that carries both students and teachers beyond the dimensions of their usual life.

Here is what we consider a true teacher to be: one who grasps the significance of phenomena and builds associations between life and conscience. The teacher hears the truth in everything and can express it in any language. School is like a laboratory for future generations, and the teacher is its physician. The teacher is the one who can heal our social ailments and remove the dark clouds from our horizon.

Our Philosophy of Education (II)[11]

Learning and teaching are two of humanity's lofty duties. The merits of education unearth our soul's capacities and fashion us into models of civility. Virtues cannot develop in individuals who have not been purified by education, nor is it useful to look to them for social loyalty.

But this raises important questions: What should we learn and what should we not learn? What should we teach and when should we teach it? Knowledge that is offered at the wrong time is like a fog that shrouds the mind. This kind of knowledge does not give light to its possessor and hence cannot benefit others. Although knowledge is valuable in itself, many times it can become a burden. To desire to know everything, or to seek knowledge for its own sake, leaves us with nothing but a barrage of mere information.

Education should help students integrate their personalities and discover the relationship between the external world and their inward experience. All knowledge should provide us with a sound basis for action and guide us to new syntheses. The kind of knowledge that does not address the mysterious relationship between humanity and nature will not contribute to our true understanding of existence or encourage our integration with it. Science of this kind only condemns our conscience with riddles. But the harmony between the perception and interpretation of the natural world gives conscience the freedom to fulfill its purpose.

It is dangerous to desire to know everything, given that some knowledge leads to harmful consequences. Instead of striving to become information addicts, we should direct our passion toward knowledge that facilitates our integration with the universe. This attitude is the origin of genuine thinking and the clearest sign that the true spirit of learn-

---

[11] Gülen, M. Fethullah, "Bizim Maarifimiz - II," *Sızıntı*, November 1979, Issue 10; Kurt, Erkan M., *A Fethullah Gülen Reader: So That Others May Live*, New Jersey: Blue Dome Press, 2013, pp. 121–124.

ing is present in us. To approach education in this spirit is to reject rote learning and mindless memorization. Then, we will not be deceived by mere appearances or mistake the peel of existence for the fruit.

Curiosity in everything, the indiscriminate desire for knowledge, is an obstacle to serious study. True thought only engages what is necessary. The things we learn needlessly, out of idle curiosity, can be harmful to our mind and heart, and especially harmful to the pure souls of youth.

When teaching the youth, we should help them see the meaning beyond appearances. In this practice, their age and sophistication should be taken into account, for children should not be given more than they can digest. In elementary school, for instance, children should not be put under the burden of the complicated subjects of world geography, human history, or philosophy. This would only instill in them doubts and hesitations.

It is impossible to comprehend the totality of our time: the infinite unfolding of events, the countless subjects of study, and the constant developments of research. Any attempt at such comprehension is clearly futile. Our time requires the division of labor, distribution of duties, and specialization. Students should devote themselves to a small part of the field of knowledge and seek to fulfill their role as students within that specialty.

Today, the family and social environment fail to motivate youth toward these educational ideals; the nobility of their inwardness is neglected. Their souls learn only the deadly lessons of their environment. In this context, they are not likely to preserve their original purity. The trifles of daily news, the endless games of political polemics, entertainment predicated on lies, deception, and sensation completely occupy their young minds. Even the heroes of spirituality could not endure such a burden! It is only natural, given the nature of these distractions, that youth struggle to understand the lessons of school, integrate them into their life, and achieve wisdom.

Today's students have been made lazy by a corrupt culture, and they pursue only what can be had with little effort. Pop culture preoccupies them with worthless goals and exploits their youthful fancies.

In this context, it is incredibly difficult to teach them what it means to truly accomplish greatness. They find labor and exertion displeasing and will not endure systematic study. How can we cultivate virtue in youth whose minds are plagued daily by trivialities and whose hearts are wasted in meaningless struggles? If their animal instincts and lustful desires are encouraged every day, how will they find the strength to read and reflect?

The knowledge of goodness resists corruption and degeneration. The youth will receive this power first from the school of their teachers, then from the greater school of life. Only when they are equipped with this transcendent knowledge will they gain the strength to resist evils and rise on the wings of their will. On the other hand, the lack of this knowledge will leave the youth impotent and defenseless, and the knowledge of evil will paralyze them.

It is sad that more people do not take a stand against this social crisis or mobilize their resources to overcome it.

What Education Promises[12]

The happiness of a nation can only be sustained if new generations are raised up in the integrity of both heart and mind. But the youth of our time have been born into inauspicious bosoms of neglect. They find themselves in the midst of ruthless leaders, deadly ideologues, and debilitating media. It is our responsibility to rescue youth from this suffocating atmosphere, for it is their dynamic potential that will create for us a future. We must teach them how to exist by their own will: This is the sacred mission of all authorities and administrators.

We entrust our future to the youth. If they cannot acquire discernment through education, they will be crushed under the weight of base instincts and bad habits. Lust, rage, and greed will separate them from the essence of their humanity and enslave them to false convictions.

[12] Gülen, M. Fethullah, "Maarifin Vaad Ettikleri," *Sızıntı*, March 1984, Issue 62; Kurt, Erkan M., *A Fethullah Gülen Reader: So That Others May Live*, New Jersey: Blue Dome Press, 2013, pp. 125–128.

According to modern pedagogy, such feelings can exert a powerful influence, even on the most educated youth, forcing them into error.

In reality, our human desires have been given to us because they can be enlisted in the service of good. Education teaches us to manage these feelings: We are fortified against their negative influences and able to direct them toward proper ends. Education teaches us how to employ even apparently harmful human emotions toward the goal of perfection. It enables the individual to develop the sense of virtue, the strength of will, the capacity for reflection, and the love of freedom that is service to the Truth.

The young generations suffer in the clutches of desire and ambition. If we fail to provide them with an education that addresses their true inwardness, if we fail to reveal to them the ways of morality and virtue, our nation will not escape its present turmoil. Obviously, nations that have successfully imparted to their young the nobility of ethics and culture will find in the new generation the guardians of sacred values; thus, their future is secure. But when nations neglect the moral and intellectual education of their children, they abandon their society to decadence and chaos.

Education should be among the primary concerns of nations, since it is so closely related to their vitality and longevity. It is even more important for a nation facing social and economic depression. In such a time of crisis, a society will be ruined if it does not diagnose its own predicament with clear eyes. If the nation obeys emotion rather than reason, if it gives in to despair or loses its way in the turbulence of the crowds, it will falter. Even the slightest errors in the matter of national education can result in enormous destruction. For all social crises, which scatter the individuals like the autumn leaves, could be said to originate in the lack of education and culture. If our national leaders cannot understand the significance of education and address instead thousands of inessential problems, then we must ask God for more patience as we wait for our Heracles.[13]

---

[13] Heracles is an image in Gülen's writings. Adopting from the Greek mythology, Gülen uses this image to refer to the heroic altruism of his ideal person of service.

Today, we face a challenge more serious and more delicate than any other. We must teach our spiritual heritage to new generations and rescue them from alienation. Our efforts in the name of education will result in our future security and happiness, whereas our negligence and indifference will culminate in misery. Therefore, as responsible people, we must review the causes of our current social disorder and develop an objective plan for enlightening our children. This is the only way to save our country and nation.

We must raise generations who comprehend their time, who are able to consider the past, present, and future together. Otherwise, God forbid, our nation will be crushed in the merciless gears of history. Just as species become extinct when they fail to adapt to their environment, nations also pass away when they do not respond to the demands of their age. They surrender the field to other, more capable nations. The ruins of past civilizations and the fossils of extinct creatures both illustrate this divine principle.

The Egyptian civilization, the Roman Empire, the Andalusian culture, the Ottoman Empire: all were crushed by the same grim reality. They survive only as withered traces or ethnographic relics! The same fate awaits every nation that does not encourage its young to cultivate in themselves systematic thinking, willpower, and the love of God. These ideals will preserve them from indolence, discouragement, and panic, will inspire them to work with enthusiasm, and will evoke in them a public spirit.

Today we have to rethink our system of education in response to the social context of our time. We need to chart a new course from the past to present and from present to future, developing clear educational guidelines for new generations. In this regard, public authorities have a special responsibility. Until the day that vigorous minds and passionate hearts face up to this problem, how can we have confidence in the future of our country, or expect our nation to be elevated?

What to Expect from Education[14]

How should we raise up the new generations? What should we teach them, and why? And who is to fulfill this sacred duty? If we are to deal with the challenges of education, we must find persuasive answers to these questions. For a system of education without a clearly defined purpose will only confuse its students. Without method, teachers can only turn their students into empty vessels of information.

A nation's social structure is intimately related to its educational system: Society takes shape according to the education of its individuals. There is more than just the immediate future at stake, for the generations we raise today are likely to raise their children according to the same method. Just as marriage and reproduction are critical for a nation's physical existence, education is vital to its spiritual and moral existence. If the nation does not secure the institution of marriage, it cannot hope to survive. Likewise, unless nations give due importance to the spiritual and moral education of society, they will not escape downfall.

In a society, individuals influence the culture, and the culture plays an important role in shaping the individual. As the head of a family exerts great influence over its members, so too does the leader of a nation over its citizens. The elevation of a nation depends on the intellectual and spiritual culture that exists among its individuals and on the insightful and truthful service of the governing body. While administrators should work sincerely for the good of the public, the latter are also expected to endeavor to attain a role within society. This reciprocity reflects the Prophetic teaching: "All of you are shepherds, and all of you are responsible for those under your care." It also complies with the high ethical preference for social prosperity over personal prosperity.

Anyone involved in raising the younger generations, no matter their title, should not forget the responsibility that comes with this

---

[14] Gülen, M. Fethullah, "Nesillerin Maariften Bekledikleri," *Sızıntı*, April 1984, Issue 63; Kurt, Erkan M., *A Fethullah Gülen Reader: So That Others May Live*, New Jersey: Blue Dome Press, 2013, pp. 129–130.

great task. As parents, we do our best to ensure a future for our children. We confront troubles and endure hardships so they can prosper. We work hard to prepare a paradise-like world for them. But if we fail to offer them the true prosperity of morality and virtue, will our effort not be wasted? A nation's greatest wealth is its culture of morality and virtue, and this capital accumulates only in the bosom of education. If a nation obtains this wealth, it will possess the power to conquer worlds and the key to the treasures of the universe. On the other hand, those masses deprived of it will lose their resources and be eliminated in life's struggle.

If we succeed in adorning the minds of the youth with the sciences of their time and instilling in their hearts the divine virtues, if we can teach them to view the future through the prism of history, our efforts will not have been in vain. Instead, we will reap much in return: Every penny spent on education of the youth will return to us as the wealth of cultured souls. As a nation, these will be our interminable treasures. For the well-educated generations will surmount all obstacles, will overcome all difficulties, whether material or spiritual, and will never fall into despair. They will not squander their spiritual inheritance; they will not know emptiness, hesitancy, or pessimism; they will not know misery.

Today, we are at a crossroads. We can either elevate our children to the truth of their humanity or abandon them to alienation. With this heavy responsibility on our shoulders, we must develop a program to reverse the decay brought about by past neglect. Otherwise, as the most precious gems of their existence begin to erode, the youth will lose sight of life's true value. They will cease to exist in their own distinct essence and will not be able to return to the glory of their past.

References

Acar, E. (2011). Effects of social capital on academic success: A narrative syntesis. *Educational Research and Review, 6*(6), 456-461. Retirived from http://www.academicjournals.org/err/

Agai, B. (2005). Discoursive and organizational strategies of the Gülen movement. Paper presented at *the International Conference on Islam in the Contemporary World: The Fethullah Gülen Movement in Thought and Practice.* Houston TX: Rice University. Retirived from http://en.fgulen.com/conference-papers/

Akyol, H. (2008). An alternative approach to preventing ethnic conflict: The role of the Gülen's schools in strengthening the delicate relations between Turkey and the Iraqi Kurds with particular reference to the "Kirkuk Crisis". Paper presented at *the International Conference on Islam in the age of global challenges: Alternative perspectives of the Gülen movement.* Washington, DC: Georgetown University. Retirived from http://en.fgulen.com/conference-papers/

Aras, B. & Caha, O. (2000). Fethullah Gülen and his liberal "Turkish Islam" movement. *Middle East Review of International Affairs, 4*(4), 30-42. Retirived from http://meria.idc.ac.il/

Aslandogan, Y. A. & Cetin, M. (2007). The philosophy of Gülen in thought and practice. In R. Hunt, & A. Y. Aslandogan, *Muslim Citizens of Globalized World* (pp. 55-74). NJ: The Light Publishing & IID Press.

Bankston, C. L. (2004). Social capital, cultural values, immigration, and academic achievement: The host country context and contradictory consequences, *Sociology of Education, 77*(2), 176-179.

Borne, M. E. (2008, Jan. 22). *Ceux qui font ecole a part.* Le Monde.

Cainkar, L. A. (2009). *Homeland insecurity: The Arab American and Muslim American experience after 9/11.* New York. NY: Russell Sage Foundation.

Can, E. (1995, August. 13-23). *Fethullah Gülen Hocaefendi ile Ufuk Turu.* Istanbul: Zaman.

Center for the Prevention of School Violence North Carolina Department of Juvenile Justice and Delinquency Prevention. (2011). *Just What is "School Violence"?* Retrieved 06, 01, 2011, from http://www.ncdjjdp.org/cpsv/pdf_files/newsbrief5_02.pdf

Cetin, M. (2010). *The Gülen movenet: Civic service without borders* . New York. NY: Blue Dome Press.

Chittick, W. C. (1999). Introduction to sufism. In R. Baker, & G. Henry, *Merton & Sufism: The Untold Story* (pp. 12-35). Lousville, KY: Fons Vitae.

Cohen, L. M. (1999). *Educational Philosophies*. Retrieved 08, 01, 2010, from http://oregonstate.edu/instruct/ed416/PP3.html

Cohen, D. & Prusak, L. (2001). *In good company. How social capital makes organizations work*. Boston, MA: Harvard Business School Press.

Coleman, S. J. (1988). Social capital in the creation of human capital. *The American Journal of Sociology, 94*, (supplement) 95-120.

Creswell, J. W. (2003). *Research design: Qualitative, quantitative, and mixed methods approaches*. Thousand Oaks, CA: Sage Publications.

Dika, S.L. & Singh, K. (2002). Applications of social capital in educational literature: A critical synthesis. *Review of Educational Research, 72*(1), 31-60.

Ebaugh, H. R. (2009). *The Gülen movement: A sociological analysis of a civic movement rooted in moderate Islam*. New York. NY: Springer.

Erdogan, L. (1996). *Kucuk dunyam*. Istanbul: Dogan Yayincilik.

Ergene, E. (2006). *Tradition witnessing the modern age: An analysis of the Gülen movement*. Somerset. New Jersey: Tugra Books

Field, J. (2003). Civic engagement and lifelong learning: Survey findings on social capital and attitudes towards learning. *Studies in the Education of Adults, 35*(2), 142-156.

Fredland, N. (2008). Nurturing hostile environments: The problem of school violence. *Family and Community Health, 31*(1S), 32-41.

Gokcek, M. (2005). Gülen and Sufism. Paper presented at *the International Conference on Islam in the Contemporary World: The Fethullah Gülen Movement in Thought and Practice*. Houston TX: Rice University. Retirived from http://en.fgulen.com/conference-papers/

Gülen, F. (1996). *Toward the lost paradise*. Ali Unal, trans. London: Truestar.

Gülen, F. (1999). *Key concepts in the practice of sufism*. Ali Unal, trans. Fairfax, VA: The Fountain.

Gülen, F. (2000a). *Pearls of wisdom*. Ali Unal, trans. Fairfax, Virginia: The Fountain

Gülen, F. (2000b). *Essays, perspectives, opinions*. Fairfax, Virginia: The Fountain

Gülen, F. (2004a). *Toward a global civilization of love & tolerance*. Mehmet Unal, Nagihan Haliloglu, Mukerrem Fanikucukmehmedoglu, trans. New Jersey: The Light Inc.

Gülen, F. (2004b). *Love and the essence of being human*. Mehmet Unal, Nilufer Korkmaz, trans. Istanbul, Turkey: Journalists and Writers Foundation Publications.

Gülen, F. (2005). *The statue of our souls: Revival in Islamic thought and activism.* Muhammed Cetin, trans. New Jersey: The Light Inc.

Gutek, G. L. (2011). *Historical and philosophical foundations of Education* (5th ed.). New York. NY: Pearson.

Hermansen, M. (2005). Understanding of "community" within the Gülen movement. Paper presented at *the International Conference on Islam in the Contemporary World: The Fethullah Gülen Movement in Thought and Practice.* Houston TX: Rice University. Retirived from http://en.fgulen.com/conference-papers/

Horvat, E. M., Weininger, E. B. & Lareau, A. (2003). From social ties to social capital: Class differences in the relations between schools and parent networks. *American Educational Research Journal, 40*(2), 319–351.

Irvine, J. (2007). The Gülen movement and Turkish integration in Germany. In R. Hunt, & Y. A. Aslandogan, *Muslim Citizens of Globalized World* (pp. 55-74). NJ: The Light Publishing & IID Press.

Kalyoncu, M. (2008). *A civilian response to ethno-religious conflict: The gülen movement in southeast Turkey.* New York: The Light Publishing.

Kim, H. (2005). F. Gülen and Sufism: A Contemporary Manifestation of Sufism. Paper presented at *the International Conference on Islam in the Contemporary World: The Fethullah Gülen Movement in Thought and Practice.* Houston TX: Rice University. Retirived from http://en.fgulen.com/conference-papers/

Lutheran Schools of America, (n.d). *Lutheran Schools of America.* Retrieved 11 04, 2010 from http://www.lsaels.org

Marlow, E. (1992). Philosophy of teaching in the junior college. (ERIC Document Reproduction Service No: ED 354 539) Retrieved August 29, 2010, from EBSCOHost ERIC database.

Marlow, E. (1996). Philosophy of teaching mathematics. (ERIC Document Reproduction Service No: ED 402 162) Retrieved August 29, 2010, from EBSCOHost ERIC database.

McDermott, E. J. (1997). Distinctive qualities of Catholic school. Second Edition. NCEA Keynote Series. Washington DC: National Catholic Educational Association. (ERIC Document Reproduction Service No: ED 410 669) Retrieved June 29, 2010, from EBSCOHost ERIC database.

Mehmeti, J. (2009). The role of education in Kosovo: The contribution of the Gülen movement. Paper presented at the *International Conference of East and West Encounters: The Gülen Movement.* Los Angeles, CA: University of Southern California.

Merriam, S. B. & Associates (2002). *Qualitative research in practice: Examples for discussion and analysis.* San Francisco. CA: Jossey-Bass Publishers.

Michel, T. (2005). Fethullah Gülen as educator. Paper presented at the *second international conference on Islam in the contemprorary world: The Gülen movement in thought and practice.* Houston. TX: Rice University.

Noddings, N. (2007). *Philosophy of education.* CO: Westview Press.

Ozdalga, E. (2003). Following in the footsteps of Fethullah Gülen: Three women teachers tell their stories. In Yavuz, H & Esposito, J. *Turkish islam and the secular state: The Gülen movement* (pp. 85-114). NY: Syracuse University.

Ozkok, E. (1995, January. 23-30). *Müslümanlığı her yanıyla bilmeliyiz.* Istanbul: Hürriyet.

Patton, M. Q. (1990). *Qualitative evaluation and research methods* (2nd ed.). Newbury Park, CA: Sage Publications, Inc.

Santos, S. L. (2006). The urgency of educational reform in the United States of America: Lessons learned from Fethullah Gülen. Paper presented at *Second International Conference on Islam in the Contemporary World: The Fethullah Gülen Movement in Thought and Practice.* University of Oklahoma, Norman, OK.

Tavernise, S. (2008, May 04). *Turkish schools offer Pakistan a gentler vision of Islam.* New York: New York Times.

Unal, A. & Williams, A. (2000). *Advocate of dialog.* Fairfax Virginia: Fountain.

Williams, I. G. (2005). An absent influence? The Gülen movement in Turkish-Islam and its influence on global education and inter-religious dialogue. Paper presented at *the International Conference on Islam in the Contemporary World: The Fethullah Gülen Movement in Thought and Practice.* Houston TX: Rice University. Retirived from http://en.fgulen.com/conference-papers/

Woodhall, R. (2005). Organizing the organization, educating the educators: An examination of Fethullah Gülen's teaching and the membership of the movement. Paper presented at *the Conference of Islam in the Contemporary World: The Fethullah Gülen Movement in Thought and Practice,* Houston, TX: Rice University. Retirived from http://en.fgulen.com/conference-papers/

Yavuz, H. (2003). The Gülen Movement. In H. Y. Esposito. *Turkish Islam and the secular state: The Gülen movement* (pp. 19-47). New York. NY: Syracuse University Press.

Yavuz, H. (2004, July 21). The Gülen movement: A modern expression of Turkish Islam. (Religioscope, Interviewer).